# Developing Vocabulary Skills

## Second Edition

# Dennis Keen

## Spokane Community College

**HEINLE & HEINLE PUBLISHERS**
*A Division of Wadsworth, Inc.*
*Boston, Massachusetts 02116 U.S.A.*

The publication of *Developing Vocabulary Skills,* Second Edition, was directed by the members of the Global Innovations Publishing Team at Heinle & Heinle:

David C. Lee, Editorial Director
Gabrielle B. McDonald, Production Editor

Also participating in the publication of this program were:

| | |
|---|---|
| Publisher: | Stanley J. Galek |
| Editorial Production Manager: | Elizabeth Holthaus |
| Project Manager: | Judy Keith |
| Assistant Editor: | Kenneth Mattsson |
| Associate Marketing Manager: | Donna Hamilton |
| Production Assistant: | Maryellen Eschmann |
| Manufacturing Coordinator: | Mary Beth Lynch |
| Photo Coordinator: | Martha Leibs-Heckly |
| Interior Designer: | Sue Gerould, Perspectives |
| Page Layout: | Christine E. Wilson, IBC |
| Cover Illustrator: | Jean Tuttle; Illustration © Jean Tuttle 1993 |
| Cover Designer: | Kimberly Wedlake |

Photo Credits: p. 36, David Wells/Image Works; p. 37, Owen Franken/Stock, Boston; p. 84, Alon Reininger/Contact Press Images; pp. 85, 120, 121, 237, AP/Wide World Photos; p. 168, Bernard Bisson/Stock, Boston; p. 169, Ulrike Welsch; p. 238, Cary S. Wolinsky/Stock, Boston.

Heinle & Heinle Publishers is a division of Wadsworth, Inc.

Manufactured in the United States of America

Library of Congress Cataloging-in-Publication Data

Keen, Dennis.
    Developing vocabulary skills / Dennis Keen.—2nd ed.
    p.      cm.
    ISBN 0-8384-4672-8
    1. Vocabulary.   2. English language—Textbooks for foreign
speakers.   I. Title
PE1449.K34   1992
428.1—dc20                                      93-38689
                                                        CIP

ISBN:  0-8384-4672-8

10 9 8 7 6 5 4

For Elizabeth

May she always love words

# Contents

# Preface: To the Student

There are many ways to build up your English vocabulary. You can read books and magazines in English, write down all the words you do not know, and then look them up in your dictionary. You could choose to memorize five or ten new words a day. You could write frequently, and in choosing a variety of words, your vocabulary would increase. You might choose a word like **happy** and learn the words similar in meaning, such as **gleeful**, **joyful**, **jovial**, and **ebullient**. You might also learn the words and phrases often used with **happy**, such as **happy birthday**, **happy-go-lucky**, and **money-happy**. And you might further learn the opposites of **happy**: **sad**, **morose**, and **tearful**.

All of these ways will help, but this book looks at vocabulary development in a different way. English can be a very difficult language to learn, and one of the reasons for this is the size of its vocabulary. English has, according to some counts, over 200,000 words although one very large dictionary, *The Oxford English Dictionary,* has over 500,000 entries. English has far more words than most other languages. For example, French has only about 100,000. Fortunately, many words in English are related by common roots or bases and learning these roots unlocks the meaning to many English terms. In this book, you will learn the roots and affixes (these terms will be defined later) that are common to the words found in college texts and academic writing.

For example, a common root in English is *prim,* meaning "first, or most important." When we see this root, we can often (but not always) guess that the word means something about "first or most important." Thus, learning *prim* helps you guess at the meanings of **prime** (something important), **primer** (a first coat of paint or the first book one learns to read), **premiere** (the first showing of a movie or play), and **primary colors** (the three most important colors).

One problem with this method is that it does not always work. The term **prim** by itself means "neat" and **to primp** means to "dress carefully." English is not like mathematics or the sciences; few rules in English are always true, and language changes in ways that math and science do not. In learning English vocabulary, you need to make intelligent, thoughtful guesses. More importantly, you need to get ready for some messiness. You need to be patient.

Here, then, is a good system to use with the exercises and readings in *Developing Vocabulary Skills:*

Step 1: When you come across a word you do not know, ANALYZE the word. To ANALYZE a word is to break the word down into its parts—its prefixes, suffixes, and roots. For example, **incorrect** has three parts: **in + cor + rect**, and the three parts mean: "not + totally + right." You will need to use the Glossary of this book often to find the meanings of roots and affixes. Students who make regular use of the back of the book will find that their word knowledge grows quickly.

Step 2: After you have ANALYZED a word, form a LITERAL DEFINITION of it. The analysis goes on in your mind; the literal definition goes down on your paper. That is the only difference. The LITERAL DEFINITION of **incorrect** is "not completely right."

Step 3: Once you have a LITERAL DEFINITION, you test that definition in the sentence before you: "Your answers to Questions 16 and 37 are incorrect." If "not completely right" makes sense for **incorrect** as it is used in the sentence, you have done all that you need to do.

Step 4: Sometimes the LITERAL DEFINITION will not seem to fit the meaning of the word in the sentence. For example, look at the following problem:

| | |
|---|---|
| Term: | **primitive** |
| Analysis: | prim + ive |
| Literal Definition: | related to + first |
| Sentence: | Primitive people drew pictures on cave walls. |

If you use a LITERAL DEFINITION for **primitive**, you would write: "related to the first"; however, "very early or very ancient" is a definition that seems to fit better. Often, you may have to change the LITERAL DEFINITION to fit the sentence. This new definition is called the CONTEXTUAL DEFINITION, the meaning that makes sense in the context or setting of a sentence.

In summary, here are the steps:

ANALYZE the word in your mind.
Create a LITERAL DEFINITION with the help of your Glossary.
Test the LITERAL DEFINITION in the sentence.
If you so need, create a CONTEXTUAL DEFINITION to fit the sentence.

As with learning any new skill, this process will seem odd and hard at first, but do keep working the system. Once you use the steps regularly, you will find that your understanding of words grows quickly. In fact, make the method your primary way of thinking in the units that follow.
Have fun with all the hard work before you.

Acknowledgments:

Few books are created by one person, and this one is no exception. Ken Mattsson and David Lee of Heinle and Heinle have given patience and sound advice. Heide Carlson attended to much of the word processing with skill and good humor. Bonnie Raper and Alice Clymer, of Spokane Community College, saved me hours of work and endless frustration because of their generous help with the intricacies of computers. Denise Lambert, Instructor of English at Spokane Community College, had a very good editorial eye and offered both encouragement and understanding throughout the revision process. Finally, hundreds of students have worked through the first edition of the text, and their comments and criticisms have made invaluable contributions to this second edition. The strengths of the book arise in goodly measure from the efforts and thoughts of these people.

I would also like to thank the following people whose comments helped me in the development of the second edition: Susan Applefeld, College of Notre Dame of Maryland; Hollace Beard-Hunting, University of Arkansas at Little Rock; Patricia Brenner, University of Washington; Nelia I. Camargo, Brooklyn College; Piero Carlini, Cambria English Institute; Marta O. Dmytrenko-Ahrabian, Wayne State University; Kimbrough Ernest, ELS San Francisco; Catherine Mason, ELS St. Paul; Monica Maxwell-Paegle, Georgetown University; Bruce McCutcheon, University of Washington; Mary Frances McKay, ELS St. Paul; K. Newcomer, University of Washington; Lynne Nickerson, DeKalb College; Marshall Palmer, University of Washington; Derek W. Streeter, ELS St. Paul; Bart Weyand, University of Southern Maine; Joyce Wulff, Cambria English Institute; Rosemarie Zannino, College of Notre Dame of Maryland.

# I

# Introduction to Word Analysis

# 1 Compound Words

A compound word is the simplest word to analyze, for all compound words are made up of two separate yet common words. For example, **newspaper** is created by joining **news + paper**; the word means "a paper with news printed in it." In the same way, a **bookstore** is a "store that sells books." And you might create a sentence like this with several compound words: "Each **weekday**, I buy a **newspaper outside** the **bookstore downtown**."

You will often find analysis of words easier if you break them down and define the parts backwards, from the last element to the first. For example, a **headache** is "a pain in your head," and **backyard** is the "yard in back of the house."

## WORD LIST

| | | | |
|---|---|---|---|
| afternoon | baseball | birthday | bookcase |
| carload | cloudburst | crosswalk | dropout |
| earring | earthquake | headline | highway |
| homework | housework | landslide | paperback |
| sidewalk | skateboard | spacecraft | tugboat |
| woodland | | | |

# Analysis

Analyze each of the following words, and write a literal definition on the line. Then write one sentence that includes both compound words. The first one has been done for you.

1. skateboard: _a board on which you skate_

   sidewalk: _a walk beside the street_

   Sentence: _Please do not ride your skateboard on the sidewalk._

2. cloudburst: _____

   landslide: _____

   Sentence: *The cloudburst covered landslide.*

3. homework: _____

   housework: *Mona does not have homework, but*

   Sentence: *she has housework.*

4. afternoon: _____

   birthday: _____

   Sentence: *This afternoon we have birthday party.*

5. highway: _____

   earring: _____

   Sentence: *She droped her earring on the highway.*

# Relationships

I. The word **ball** appears in the name of many sports. Look at the following compound words and explain how the first part of the compound word is connected to the sport. The first one has been done for you.

   1. baseball: *a game in which runners run to or around bases*

   2. football: _____

   3. basketball: _____

   4. volleyball: _____

   5. softball: _____

II. Where would you expect to find or see the following?

   1. carload: _____

   2. headline: _____

   3. crosswalk: _____

   4. woodland: _____

3

5. spacecraft: _____

6. bookcase: _____

# Collaborative Work

I.   Read the paragraph below, circle all the compound words, and answer the questions that follow.

As I sat in the classroom waiting for my first college class to begin, I felt both surprise and fear. My fellow classmates seemed so calm, so casual. Barefooted, the students wore baggy sweatshirts and shorts. I saw haircuts of every type, footwear of every description, and earrings beyond belief. All through my schooling, I wore one boring uniform and one equally boring hairstyle. Such a variety here was a pleasant surprise. Yet the students were both relaxed and serious. Some were reading textbooks; some were writing in their notebooks. I was sure every student was smarter than I was; I was certain they would not struggle with the homework. All was new; all was exciting. I was very glad to begin.

1.   List all the compound words from the paragraph that you do not know.

_____     _____

_____     _____

_____     _____

_____     _____

2.   Was the writer's experience anything like your first day at a new school? In what ways were the first days alike? In what ways were they different?

_____

_____

_____

_____

_____

_____

3.  In groups or with a partner, compare your list of words in question 1. Find some-one who knows the words you do not know, and ask him or her to explain them to you. In return, explain to others the listed terms that they do not know.

4.  Compare your answers to question 2 by reading your responses to your partner or group.

II.  Most compound words are made up of two short words. In a group, list at least three compound words that use each of the following words.

**EXAMPLE:   ball: gumball, ballpark, ballgame, softball, football, basketball**

1.  air: _____

2.  head: _____

3.  down: _____

4.  sun: _____

5.  water: _____

6.  tail: _____

# 2 Familiar Prefixes and Suffixes

English contains thousands of words, but very few of them are compounds. Most words are more difficult to analyze. However, many longer words in English have word parts and can be analyzed in the same way you analyze compound words.

Words in English are formed by adding affixes to roots. A *root* is either a base word or a group of letters with a special meaning. An *affix* is a group of letters, again with a special meaning, that is attached to the front or back of a root.

For example, **work** is a good English word and root. We can use it to form compound words, such as:

**homework, housework, schoolwork, workshop, workday**

But we can also add affixes to the root or base word.

| | | |
|---|---|---|
| **re- (again)** | **re + work** | **re**work** the problem** |
| **-able (can do)** | **work + able** | **a work**able** solution** |
| **un- (not)** | **un + work + able** | **an un**work**able solution** |
| **-er (one who)** | **work + er** | **a wor**k**er in the factory** |

The affixes above (**re-**, **-able**, **un-** and **-er**) are groups of letters that have a meaning, but they generally cannot be words by themselves. If the affix is at the beginning of a root word, it is called a *prefix;* if at the end, it is called a *suffix.*

## WORD LIST

**re-: again**

**Example:** **Please rewrite your paper. (write again)**

| | | |
|---|---|---|
| **rebuild** | **recede** | **remarry** |
| **revise** | **rewrite** | |

**re-: back**

**Example:** **I need to rewind the tape. (wind or turn back)**

| | | |
|---|---|---|
| **repay** | **repel** | **replay** |
| **retract** | **rewind** | |

**-less**: without

**Example:**    Homeless people fill the city. (without a place to live)

| homeless | limitless | senseless |
| sleepless | stainless | |

**-ful**: full of, covered with

**Example:**    I slept a restful sleep. (full of rest or peace)

| beautiful | forgetful | grateful |
| restful | thankful | |

**-able** (**-ible**):    can, can do

**Example:**    I have a portable radio. (able to be carried)

| breakable | legible | portable |
| tangible | taxable | |

**-ly**: in a way that is . . .

**Example:**    I slowly sank into bed. (in a way that is slow)

| amply | correctly | gradually |
| perfectly | slowly | |

# Analysis

I.    Analyze and write a literal definition for the following words. Then, on a separate sheet of paper, write a sentence for each one. The first definition has been done for you.

1.   remarry:   _marry or wed_      _again_

2.   repay: _____   _____

3.   senseless: _____   _____

4.   beautiful: _____   _____

5.   breakable: _____   _____

6.   perfectly: _____   _____

II.  With a compound word, your analysis gives you two words: **barcode** means, literally, "a code formed by bars." The literal definition can be expanded to better fit the meaning in the sentence: "a code written in bar form on the bottom or sides of packages," as in the sentence "The cashier scanned a barcode." With some familiar prefixes, the analysis gives you a prefix and a word: **redo** means "do again." Most often, however, the analysis will not give you words; it will give you roots and affixes.

For example, the word **repel** is in the Word List. An analysis of this word gives you re + pel. _Pel_ is not a word; it is a root. A root is a word part that has a very clear meaning but is rarely itself a word. In the Word List, _pel_, _tang_, and _rect_ are all examples of roots. _Pel_ means "push," _tang_ means "touch," and _rect_ means "right."

In this book, you will need to check the Glossary quite often to find the meanings of roots and affixes. The more you use the Glossary, the stronger your vocabulary will become.

The next exercise will help you become familiar with the Glossary. First, analyze the **boldface** term in each sentence. You will find a root, but you will probably not know what the root means. Look up that root in the Glossary. The root's meaning and your knowledge of the affix will combine to give you a good literal definition of the word. Write that definition on the line. The first one has been done for you.

1.  The tide **recedes** in the afternoon. My hairline is **receding**.

    Root: _cede_     Meaning: _move_

    **Recede:** _move back_

2.  She **revived** the dying patient. The artist **revived** the style.

    Root: _____     Meaning: _____

    **Revive:** _____

3.  Put the car in **reverse**. **Reverse** the trend of senseless murder.

    Root: _____     Meaning: _____

    **Reverse:** _____

4.  The spray will **repel** insects. I was **repelled** by its ugliness.

    Root: _____     Meaning: _____

    **Repel:** _____

5.  **Regardless** of the danger facing her, the officer rushed into the house. I will go, **regardless** of what you say or think. (Note: the term has a root and two affixes.)

    Root: _____     Meaning: _____

**Regardless:** _____

6. Is water a **limitless** resource? The skateboarder seems to have **limitless** energy.

   Root: _____ Meaning: _____

   **Limitless:** _____

7. She was **grateful** for the plateful of food. Let us be **grateful** for living through the earthquake.

   Root: _____ Meaning: _____

   **Grateful:** _____

8. The rice crop was **plentiful** this year. Bugs are **plentiful** in the woodlands this summer.

   Root: _____ Meaning: _____

   **Plentiful:** _____

9. Feelings are not **tangible**. A ring is often a **tangible** sign of love.

   Root: _____ Meaning: _____

   **Tangible:** _____

10. Do you have a **portable** stove? I have a **portable** radio.

    Root: _____ Meaning: _____

    **Portable:** _____

11. He answered the question **correctly**. Although she wanted to smoke, she acted **correctly** and didn't. (Note: the term has a root and two affixes.)

    Root: _____ Meaning: _____

    **Correctly:** _____

12. Athletes are **amply** paid. He was **amply** rewarded with praise.

    Root: _____ Meaning: _____

    **Amply:** _____

# Relationships

Some words take the suffix -less, some take the suffix -ful, and some take both. For example, we may say **childless**, but **childful** is not in the language. Five of the following words take only -less, five take only -ful, and five take both. Place the affixes behind each word, ask yourself if only one or if both make sense, and then place the word in the correct column.

| bottom | care | fear | hate | harm |
|--------|------|------|------|------|
| joy | noise | peace | play | price |
| sorrow | shoe | use | worth | youth |

| -less | -ful | -less and -ful |
|-------|------|----------------|
| 1. _____ | _____ | _careless_ |
| | | _careful_ |
| 2. _____ | _____ | _____ |
| | | _____ |
| 3. _____ | _____ | _____ |
| | | _____ |
| 4. _____ | _____ | _____ |
| | | _____ |
| 5. _____ | _____ | _____ |
| | | _____ |

# Collaborative Work

I.  Many words in English often appear in pairs. **Salt and pepper, receding tide,** and **insect repellent** are just a few examples. In a group or with a partner, give a word or phrase commonly used with the following terms. The first one has been done for you.

1.  reset the    _timer or clock_____

2.  retake the   _____

3.  rewrite the  _____

4.  replay the   _____

5. rewind the _____

6. sleepless _____

7. cloudless _____

8. stainless _____

9. graceful _____

10. navigable _____

11. taxable _____

12. legible _____

II. **Sesquipedalian** is a long word that means "related to a long word." A literal definition is "related to a word that is a foot and a half long." In English, there are many
sesquipedalian words, and they often grow that long by adding affixes.

In a group or with a partner, analyze each of these terms as they grow.

1. end: stopping place

   endless: _without stopping_____

   endlessly: _____

   The mayor spoke endlessly.

2. build: make

   rebuild: _____

   rebuildable: _____

   unrebuildable: _____

   The damaged bridge was unrebuildable.

3. bear: stand, live through

   bearable: _____

   unbearable: _____

   unbearably: _____

   The weather is unbearably hot.

# 3

# Suffixes for People, Objects, and Places

Another common set of suffixes are those that mean "one who" or "something that" does an action. For example, a **teacher** is "one who teaches," a **pianist** is "one who plays piano," and a **cleaner** is "something that cleans." Closely related to these suffixes are the ones that mean "a place where."

## WORD LIST

**-er (-ar, -or): one who**

**Example:**    The **cashier** gave me change. (one who works with money)

| | | |
|---|---|---|
| baker | bystander | cashier |
| donor | dressmaker | forecaster |
| grader | lawyer | liar |
| mariner | overeater | worker |

**-er (-ar, -or): something that**

**Example:**    Put this in the **freezer.** (something that freezes food)

| | | |
|---|---|---|
| blender | chopper | cleaner |
| clipper | cracker | freezer |
| pacemaker | primer | skyscraper |
| strainer | tractor | trailer |

**-ist:   one who**

**Example:**    A **dentist** pulls teeth. (one who works with teeth)

| | | |
|---|---|---|
| artist | botanist | cyclist |
| dentist | druggist | florist |
| journalist | linguist | motorist |
| novelist | pharmacist | racist |

**-ian:  one who is skilled at**

**Example:**     The **musician** played the piano. (one skilled at music)

| | | |
|---|---|---|
| dietician | electrician | guardian |
| librarian | mathematician | mortician |
| musician | pedestrian | pediatrician |
| physician | politician | vegetarian |

**-ery (-ary, -ory):  a place where something happens or is done**

**Example:**     I need a **lavatory.** (a place to wash)

| | | |
|---|---|---|
| armory | bakery | brewery |
| diary | dormitory | factory |
| hatchery | laboratory | lavatory |
| library | memory | mortuary |

# Analysis

I.   Analyze and form a literal definition of the following compound terms and use each in a sentence. The first one has been done for you.

1.  dressmaker:  _one who makes dresses_ _____

2.  overeater: _____

3.  bystander: _____

4.  pacemaker: _____

5.  skyscraper: _____

II.  Read each of the following sentences and analyze the boldface term. You will need to use the Glossary, much as you did in Unit 2. After you have analyzed the term, answer the question.

1.  The **botanist** put on her pack and climbed into the beautiful mountains of Costa Rica, where she would study for a month.

Root: _____  Meaning: _____

What will the botanist study? _____

2. The **pharmacist** was shot during the senseless robbery.

   Root: _____ Meaning: _____

   What were the robbers trying to get? _____

3. The **mortician** gently crossed the arms of the corpse.

   Root: _____ Meaning: _____

   What happened to the person? _____

4. The **linguist** sat for hours, replaying the tapes.

   Root: _____ Meaning: _____

   What was on the tapes? _____

5. The library held a dinner to honor its major **donors.**

   Root: _____ Meaning: _____

   Why were the donors honored? _____

6. The painter chose her **primer** carefully.

   Root: _____ Meaning: _____

   What will she do with the primer? _____

7. The **pediatrician** gave his patient good advice.

   Root: _____ Meaning: _____

   Describe his patient. _____

8. The **geriatrician** gave her patient good advice.

   Root: _____ Meaning: _____

   Describe her patient. _____

9. The ancient **mariner** had a wild dream.

   Root: _____ Meaning: _____

   What was his dream about? _____

10. The tallest building on campus was the **dormitory**.

Root: _____  Meaning: _____

What is the primary purpose for a dorm? _____

# Relationships

An *analogy* is a comparison between two sets of words. In analogies, the connection between the words is emphasized. For example, we may say that a ship and a canoe are analogous or comparable because they both carry people on water.

There are four words in every analogy, and three are always given. You must put in the fourth to complete the connection. An incomplete analogy looks like this:

bird : nest :: human: _____

To do this analogy, you must figure out the connection between **bird** and **nest**. A bird builds a nest and lives in it. So what does a human build and live in? A home or a house. Thus, the completed analogy looks like this—bird : nest :: human : house.

We read this phrase: "Bird is to nest as human is to house."

Complete the following analogies, using any word that makes sense.

apple : tree :: grape :      *vine* _____

tree : bark :: banana : _____

dog : bark :: duck : _____

Complete the following analogies, using words from the Word List. The first one has been done for you.

1. aviator : airplane :: *motorist* _____ : automobile

2. director : actor :: conductor : _____

3. instructor : classroom :: scientist : _____

4. illustrator : pictures :: _____ : books

5. _____ : courtroom :: politician : capitol

6. predict : _____ :: study : analyst

7. store : _____ :: bank : teller

8. bread : _____ :: cars : factory

9. sick : physician :: overweight : _____

10. typist : office :: machinist : _____

11. children : nursery :: fish : _____

12. _____ : beer :: distillery : whiskey

13. newspaper : _____ :: public : private

14. beautician : barber :: pharmacist : _____

15. car : road :: _____ : sidewalk

# Collaborative Work

I. The following words can mean both "someone who" and "something that," depending on the sentence. On your own, write two sentences for each word to illustrate both meanings. Then, in a group or with a partner, compare your sentences and the meanings of the words.

---

**EXAMPLE:** **The baby liked to suck on the pacifier, and soon became quiet.
In our family, my aunt took the role of pacifier, always trying to keep the peace.**

1. grader _____

_____

2. printer _____

_____

3. carrier _____

_____

4. recorder _____

_____

5. cleaner _____

_____

II. In each of the groups of words below, one word does not logically fit. Find the term that does not belong, circle it, and then give a category name to the words that remain.

---

**EXAMPLE:**   pianist     organist     cellist     (equestrian)     violinist

**Category:** _musicians_____     (An equestrian is one who rides horses; all the rest are musicians.)

1. sifter     strainer     diner     toaster     roaster     blender

   Category: _____

2. freighter     glider     steamer     tanker     shrimper     trawler

   Category: _____

3. accountant     banker     bookkeeper     colonist     cashier     treasurer

   Category: _____

4. counselor     advisor     therapist     retailer     psychologist

   Category: _____

5. journalist     retailer     buyer     trader     merchant     manager

   Category: _____

6. botanist     zoologist     florist     gardener     herbalist

   Category: _____

7. comedian     magician     cartoonist     historian     humorist

   Category: _____

8. robber     burglar     arsonist     briber     survivor

   Category: _____

9. dietician     mathematician     statistician     geometrician

   Category: _____

10. monastery     seminary     rectory     apiary     sanctuary

   Category: _____

# 4 Noun Suffixes

English words fall into several grammatical classes. Verbs indicate action and time; adverbs describe verbs. Nouns are objects, beings, actions, and ideas; adjectives describe nouns.

English also has the ability to move words from one category to another by changing their endings. For example, a verb can become a noun: **select/selection**, **differ/difference**, and **measure/measurement**. Adjectives can also convert to nouns: **happy/happiness**, **able/ability**, and **hard/hardship**. Even nouns can be changed to other nouns: **child/childhood** and **friend/friendship**.

A noun suffix is very hard to define. Most mean "the act of doing something or the condition of being something," but such definitions are a bit unclear. Try to be flexible in your definitions: match the definition to the word as it is used in the sentence. Think about this sentence: "I will never forget one event in my childhood." **Childhood** could be defined as "the condition of being a child," but in this sentence a clearer meaning might be "a time when one is young."

## WORD LIST

**-ion**: the act of doing something or the state of being something

**Example:** I started the **discussion**. (the act of talking)

| | | |
|---|---|---|
| circulation | discussion | examination |
| motivation | rejection | translation |

**-ence** (**-ance**): the act of doing something or state of being something

**Example:** I have **confidence** in you. (having complete trust)

| | | |
|---|---|---|
| audience | confidence | conference |
| existence | hesitance | preference |

**-ment**: the act of doing something or the state of being something

**Example:** I found the **fragment** of glass. (a broken piece)

| | | |
|---|---|---|
| announcement | agreement | argument |
| encouragement | fragment | improvement |

# Analysis

Choose a word from the Word List to match the literal definition.  Once you have chosen a word, check your answer by looking up the word's root in the Glossary.

1.  "broken pieces" _____

   The druggist picked up the _____ of the dish.

   The journalist heard _____ of the conversation.

2.  "the desire to move toward a goal" _____

   A student who lacks _____ rarely graduates.

   I have no _____ to study tonight.

3.  "movement in circle" _____

   William Harvey discovered the _____ of blood.

   Take the book to the _____ desk of the library.

4. "having complete trust in someone or something" _____

    A mariner must have _____ in his boat.

    The politician must have _____ in her staff.

5. "being very difficult" _____

    The _____ of AIDS has prevented an easy cure.

    Both English and calculus have _____.

6. "belonging to a country" _____

    The musician held dual _____ in the U.S. and Canada.

    I will take the _____ test next month.

7. "the state of being quiet" _____

    The artist thought best in the _____ of the night.

    On test days, _____ filled the classroom.

8. "a lack of ability or skill" _____

    Throughout school, math was my strength and English my _____.

    Approaching the cliff's edge, the motorist felt a sudden _____

    in his knees.

9. "sharing the same opinion" _____

    The two nations reached a trade _____.

    The two men thought they had an _____.

10. "the change from one language to another" _____

    Some ideas were lost in the _____.

    _____ is a very hard task for me.

# Relationships

I.   Certain verbs often need to be followed by certain parts of speech. For example, we often say "He **is sad**" but rarely "He **has sadness.**" **Is** needs an adjective; **has** needs a noun. The sentences "He is sadness" and "He has sad" are rare in English.

Rewrite the following sentences, changing the boldface verbs to nouns and the boldface nouns to verbs or adjectives. Use the Glossary to help you define unknown terms and place an asterisk (*) by the sentence you feel is the clearest, which will either be the original sentence or the one you wrote.

---

**EXAMPLES:**

**There was opposition to the government plan.**

**Rewrite:** _Many people opposed the government plan._

**I like what you have created.**

**Rewrite:** _I like your creation._

1.   The linguist had **fluency** in Russian, English, and Chinese.

Rewrite: _____

2.   In many wars, one country's **invasion** of another creates mass destruction.

Rewrite: _____

3.   A challenge all nations face is to **generate** cheap, clean power for factories, offices, and homes.

Rewrite: _____

4.   The **competition** between athletes at the Olympics is fierce and strong.

Rewrite: _____

5.   The poet wrote with great **forcefulness.**

Rewrite: _____

6.   The government placed **limitations** on what novelists could publish.

Rewrite: _____

7. The laboratory was filled with **tension**.

   Rewrite: _____

8. The tanker **collided** with the freighter, creating a huge oil spill.

   Rewrite: _____

9. The class felt great **confusion** whenever verbs were discussed.

   Rewrite: _____

10. What is your **contribution** to the huge garbage problem?

   Rewrite: _____

II. Using words from the Word List, complete the following analogies.

1. _____ : live :: death : die

2. discouragement : harm :: _____ : help

3. selection : keep :: _____ : throw away

4. calculus : complexity :: arithmetic : _____

5. difference : argument :: _____ : agreement

6. director : _____ :: follower : obedience

7. visa : travel :: _____ : vote

8. pass : _____ :: fail : sadness

# Collaborative Work

Many nouns are formed from verbs. Give the base verb for each of the following nouns. Some are easy; some are hard.

1. creation / _____

2. expansion / _____

3. absorption / _____

4. adhesion / _____

5. disappearance / _____

6. hesitance / _____

7. abstinence / _____

8. detention / _____

9. achievement / _____

10. improvement / _____

11. impediment / _____

12. accompaniment / _____

13. rejection / _____

14. corrosion / _____

15. destruction / _____

# 5 Adjective Suffixes

Adjectives add information or details to nouns.

## WORD LIST

**-y**: full of or covered with

**Example:** A rose is **thorny.** (full of sharp points)

| | | |
|---|---|---|
| dirty | easy | funny |
| furry | needy | noisy |
| rocky | stormy | thorny |
| windy | | |

**-ous**: full of or covered with

**Example:** This ivy is **poisonous.** (full of poison)

| | | |
|---|---|---|
| ambitious | amorous | famous |
| humorous | joyous | nervous |
| poisonous | victorious | vigorous |
| vivacious | | |

**-al**: related to, tied to, connected with

**Example:** This is a **biennial** plant. (tied to two-year cycle)

| | | |
|---|---|---|
| accidental | biennial | coastal |
| dental | historical | legal |
| manual | natural | tribal |
| verbal | | |

**-ish**: like, similar, related to

**Example:** This plant is **grayish.** (like a gray color)

| | | |
|---|---|---|
| childish | devilish | feverish |
| foolish | grayish | Jewish |
| reddish | selfish | sluggish |
| snobbish | | |

**-ic:**  like, similar, related to

**Example:**  Seaweed is an **aquatic** plant. (related to water)

| | | |
|---|---|---|
| angelic | aquatic | Arabic |
| athletic | botanic | gigantic |
| heroic | hydraulic | poetic |
| toxic | | |

---

**-ile (-ine):**  like, similar, related to

**Example:**  This houseplant is **fragile.** (related to breaking)

| | | |
|---|---|---|
| alpine | divine | feminine |
| fertile | fragile | juvenile |
| marine | mobile | senile |
| virile | | |

---

**-ent (-ant):**  like, similar, related to

**Example:**  Lilacs are **fragrant.**  (related to smell)

| | | |
|---|---|---|
| ancient | dependent | dormant |
| evident | fragrant | pleasant |
| obedient | potent | vacant |
| valiant | | |

---

**-ive:**  causing, having power, related to

**Example:**  This plant is **attractive.** (causing a pull toward)

| | | |
|---|---|---|
| active | attractive | corrosive |
| curative | digestive | festive |
| imaginative | massive | secretive |
| talkative | | |

# Analysis

Look up the roots in the following words and write a literal definition for each.

1.  vivacious:  She was a most **vivacious** young woman.
    My **vivacious** grandmother jogs each day.

Root/Meaning: _____

Definition: _____

2. amorous: Many of Shakespeare's poems are **amorous** sonnets.
       **Amorous** thoughts filled the couple's minds.

Root/Meaning: _____

Definition: _____

3. dental: I hate **dental** examinations.
     **Dental** schools are difficult to enter, but their popularity has not decreased.

Root/Meaning: _____

Definition: _____

4. legal: I have a **legal** problem.
    These are **legal** issues of great complexity.

Root/Meaning: _____

Definition: _____

5. hydraulic: Your **hydraulic** line is split.
       **Hydraulic** power lifted the car.

Root/Meaning: _____

Definition: _____

6. toxic: **Toxic** chemicals leaked into the stream.
    No country has solved the problem of **toxic** waste.

Root/Meaning: _____

Definition: _____

7. dormant: The Peruvian volcano sat **dormant** for 300 years.
     These feelings lay **dormant** for most of my life.

Root/Meaning: _____

Definition: _____

8. senile: At ninety, my grandfather finally grew **senile**.
     Growing **senile** causes hardship for all.

Root/Meaning: _____

Definition: _____

9. juvenile: Aren't you a bit old for such **juvenile** behavior?
Their friendship seems so **juvenile**.

Root/Meaning: _____

Definition: _____

10. vacant: Why do you have such a **vacant** look on your face?
The room was **vacant**.

Root/Meaning: _____

Definition: _____

# Relationships

I.  Complete the following analogies, using terms from the Word List.

1.  smoggy : hazy :: hairy : _____

2.  rainy : sunny :: _____ : sandy

3.  heroic : courageous :: comic : _____

4.  cotton : _____ :: polyester : artificial

5.  geologic : rock :: _____ : plant

6.  _____ : taking :: generous : giving

7.  _____ : sterile :: fruitful : fruitless

8.  realistic : symbolic :: _____ : cryptic

9.  dynamite : acid :: explosive : _____

10. _____ : loquacious :: chatty : gabby

# Collaborative Work

Some of the following phrases are unusual, confusing, or wildly poetic. If the phrase clearly makes sense, write "common" on the blank and then write a sentence using the phrase. If not, write "rare" on the blank and explain why the expression is not used. Answer as many as you can on your own, bring your responses to the group, and discuss all the phrases in a group.

1. leafy cactus _____

   _____

2. angry mob _____

   _____

3. scratchy sweater _____

   _____

4. malicious saint _____

   _____

5. precious gem _____

   _____

6. voracious appetite _____

   _____

7. obedient rebel _____

   _____

8. heroic rescue _____

   _____

9. serial killer _____

   _____

10. sluggish economy _____

   _____

11. Jewish church _____

   _____

12. foolish mistake _____

   _____

13. volcanic ash _____

_____

14. atmospheric conditions _____

_____

15. chronic explosion _____

_____

16. malignant tumor _____

_____

17. pliant icicle _____

_____

18. ancient plastic _____

_____

19. a massive pebble _____

_____

20. marine desert _____

_____

21. nervous laughter _____

_____

22. competitive race _____

_____

23. stormy stillness _____

_____

24. mobile home _____

_____

25. festive funeral _____

_____

# 6 Verb Affixes

The verbs in a language usually indicate actions. Like noun suffixes, verb affixes have no exact or unchanging meaning; however, they usually mean "to make," "to have," or "to become." Once again, try to fit your definition into the meaning of the sentence.

## WORD LIST

**-ate**: to make, have, become

Example: **Terminate** printing. (to make an end)

| | | |
|---|---|---|
| abbreviate | animate | concentrate |
| graduate | liberate | regulate |
| renovate | satiate | terminate |
| tolerate | vacate | |

**en-**: to make, have, become

Example: Feet **enable** you to walk. (to make someone able)

| | | |
|---|---|---|
| enable | enamor | endanger |
| endure | engender | enliven |
| enrage | enslave | entrap |
| envision | | |

**-en**: to make, have, become

Example: **Thicken** the soup. (to make thick or less watery)

| | | |
|---|---|---|
| darken | frighten | lengthen |
| lighten | shorten | sicken |
| soften | thicken | toughen |
| weaken | | |

-ify: to make, have, become

**Example:** Milk is **fortified** with vitamins. (made stronger)

| | | |
|---|---|---|
| beautify | certify | clarify |
| falsify | fortify | gratify |
| liquify | magnify | pacify |
| rectify | unify | |

-ize: to make, have, become

**Example:** The patient **stabilized**. (to stand or stay in one place)

| | | |
|---|---|---|
| baptize | equalize | fertilize |
| legalize | memorize | minimize |
| modernize | organize | stabilize |
| standardize | | |

# Analysis

Each of the following terms has a root defined in the Glossary. Analyze the word and write a literal definition to help you understand the sentences.

1. tolerate: _____

   I cannot **tolerate** windy weather. Hardships are difficult to **tolerate**.

2. animate: _____

   The argument was **animated**. The movie was **animated**.

3. satiate: _____

   The meal **satiated** us. My senses were **satiated**.

4. envision: _____

   I **envision** a future of peace. What do you **envision** you will do next year?

5. engender: _____

   Angry words **engender** bad feelings. Try to **engender** kindness.

6. enamor: _____

   The man and woman were **enamored** with each other.
   Young men are often **enamored** with their cars.

7. clarify: _____

   The instructor **clarified** the question. Could you **clarify** what leadership means?

8. magnify: _____

   This glass will **magnify** the print. Alcohol and anger can **magnify** legal problems.

9. pacify: _____

   The food seemed to **pacify** the baby. Pol Pot could not be **pacified**.

10. fertilize: _____

    We **fertilize** the garden each year. The egg was **fertilized**.

11. memorize: _____

    There are many affixes to **memorize**.
    The visiting pianist **memorized** the sonata in a week.

12. minimize: _____

    Do not **minimize** this gigantic problem.
    His valiant action **minimized** the danger to the passengers.

13. liberate: _____

    When the nation was **liberated**, joyfulness filled the cities.
    Animal activists will sometimes **liberate** laboratory animals.

14. endure: _____

    Few people like to **endure** rejection. I **endured** the pain for three hours.

15. lengthen: _____

    After winter passes, the days **lengthen**. The instructor **lengthened** the exam.

# Relationships

Complete the following analogies, using words from the Word List.

1. dawn : brighten :: dusk : _____

2. _____ : house :: revise : essay

3. simplify : complicate :: _____ : entangle

4. elongate : lengthen :: _____ : shorten

5. heat : _____ :: cold : harden

6. germinate : ripen :: enroll : _____

7. alleviate : strengthen :: _____ : solidify

8. enclose : encage :: _____ : enchain

9. radiate : centralize :: deviate : _____

10. captivate : enchant :: _____ : madden

# Collaborative Work

Below are a few base verbs. Change these verbs to different parts of speech by adding different affixes. There may be one or more words you can make, so check with your group to see the variety.

| Verb | Noun | Adjective | One who/ Something that |
|------|------|-----------|-------------------------|
| 1. create | _____ | _____ | _____ |
| 2. argue | _____ | _____ | |
| 3. invade | _____ | _____ | _____ |
| 4. compete | _____ | _____ | _____ |
| 5. act | _____ | _____ | _____ |
| 6. imagine | _____ | _____ | |
| 7. beautify | _____ | _____ | _____ |
| 8. fertilize | _____ | _____ | _____ |
| 9. attract | _____ | _____ | |
| 10. reflect | _____ | _____ | _____ |

# Review 1

In the first six units, you were introduced to thirty important affixes. Most of them were connected to parts of speech (nouns, verbs, and adjectives). You will use these affixes over and over again in this book as you analyze and write literal definitions of new words, so now is a good time to make sure you have memorized them.

Fill in the meaning of each affix from memory, checking back to the units only for those you cannot recall. Then analyze the example word and fill in the literal definition on the right-hand line. Make sure you know these affixes before you move to *Part II: Prefixes.* Check your knowledge by testing yourself or quizzing others. Both activities will be time well spent.

## Unit 2    Familiar Prefixes and Suffixes

| Affix | Meaning | Phrase | Literal Definition |
|---|---|---|---|
| re- | _____ | **rewrite** the essay | _____ |
| re- | _____ | **rewind** the tape | _____ |
| -able | _____ | **taxable** item | _____ |
| -ful | _____ | **restful** sleep | _____ |
| -less | _____ | **homeless** people | _____ |
| -ly | _____ | drive **quickly** | _____ |

## Unit 3    Suffixes for People, Objects, and Places

| Affix | Meaning | Phrase | Literal Definition |
|---|---|---|---|
| -er | _____ | ancient **mariner** | _____ |
| -or | _____ | farm **tractor** | _____ |
| -ist | _____ | favorite **novelist** | _____ |
| -ian | _____ | brilliant **mathematician** | _____ |
| -ery | _____ | fish **hatchery** | _____ |

## Unit 4　Noun Suffixes

-ion _____ blood **circulation** _____

-ence _____ strict **confidence** _____

-ment _____ heated **argument** _____

-ness _____ **weakness** for
chocolate _____

-ship _____ financial **hardship** _____

-ity _____ product **durability** _____

## Unit 5　Adjective Suffixes

-y _____ **stormy** evening _____

-ous _____ **vigorous** growth _____

-al _____ **legal** opinion _____

-ish _____ **devilish** grin _____

-ic _____ **angelic** smile _____

-ile _____ **fertile** imagination _____

-ant _____ **dormant** volcano _____

-ive _____ **active** volcano _____

## Unit 6　Verb Suffixes

-ate _____ **tolerate** problem _____

en- _____ **endure** pain _____

-en _____ **darken** the room _____

-ify _____ **liquify** the butter _____

-ize _____ **memorize** affixes _____

# Review I: Reading

The reading selection for *Part I* contains words from the units as well as new words with the prefixes and suffixes you have learned. Analyze each of the underlined terms in the reading, using the Glossary when you need it. After you finish reading, answer the questions that follow.

## The Growth and Spread of the English Language

Millions of people all over the world study English, and a very good <u>question</u> to ask about the <u>popularity</u> of the language is: Why? Why is there a <u>preference</u> for English over other languages? What <u>historical</u> reasons can be found to <u>clarify</u> why so many people spend so many hours mastering the <u>complexity</u> of this language?

One very simple reason many people need to study English is that it seems to have an <u>endless</u> number of words. No one knows and uses all of them, but to be <u>successful</u> in many <u>academic</u> areas, you must <u>memorize</u> quite a few. If one looks at the growth of English over the last 1,500 years, one can <u>gradually</u> come to see why so many terms exist in the language.

The <u>ancient</u> <u>ancestors</u> of the English were a <u>restless</u>, <u>tribal</u> people. <u>Originally</u>, they spoke a <u>Germanic</u> tongue, but as they wandered northward from southern to northern Europe before 500 A.D., their language <u>slowly</u> changed. Most <u>importantly</u>, their vocabulary was <u>enlarged</u> each time they met speakers of other languages and borrowed words. Some languages try to <u>minimize</u> these borrowings, but English has always been able to <u>tolerate</u> many new words. For example, in these early years of English, Roman soldiers <u>donated</u> to English such words as *wine, cup, oil, rose, pillow,* and *mile.*

After the tribes <u>emigrated</u> to Britain and became Christian, their <u>conversion</u> <u>enabled</u> them to borrow from Latin such terms as *angel, priest, candle, pear,* and *pardon.* When the Norse invaded and were driven back out, they left behind words such as *skin, skull, raise,* and *screech* to <u>enliven</u> the language. Rather than try to <u>stabilize</u> the language with a small number of words, English speakers were like vacuum <u>cleaners</u>, taking in words from many other languages.

In 1066, for <u>various</u> <u>political</u> reasons,

the Normans from France conquered England, and this event changed the vocabulary <u>dramatically</u>. These "French" speaking <u>rulers</u> <u>dominated</u> the land for 150 years, <u>completely</u> changing the <u>governmental</u>, <u>legal</u> and <u>social</u>, and <u>cultural</u> life of the country. With these <u>gigantic</u> changes and <u>potent</u> new ideas came thousands and thousands of new words. In the years that followed, <u>scholars</u> and <u>writers</u> developed an interest in ancient Latin and Greek literature and philosophy, and with the <u>translations</u> of these works, thousands of more words came into the language. In fact, many of the words in this book first entered the language in the 500 years following this Norman <u>invasion</u>. And so we need to study English because of the <u>complexity</u> and size of its vocabulary, which has grown <u>steadily</u> over the centuries.

But it would be <u>foolish</u> to learn a language <u>simply</u> because it has many words. The primary reason we study English is that it has spread and is used throughout the world. At the point when the vocabulary had reached a <u>massive</u> size, at the time of Shakespeare, English spread to America, where it became the tongue of the <u>political</u> and <u>cultural</u> life of the young nation. And as the <u>British</u> Commonwealth grew in later centuries, English was carried to many <u>portions</u> of North America, Africa, Asia, and Australia. This commonwealth was once a <u>mighty</u> empire, and while its power has <u>fragmented</u>, its <u>linguistic</u> <u>influence</u> remains <u>vital</u>.

In the twentieth century, the spread of English continued. In World War II, English-speaking <u>soldiers</u> were sent all over the globe, and English was heard everywhere. As the world rebuilt itself after the hardship of war, the technical and economic strength of English-speaking nations helped many countries develop. The growth of multinational companies and television also helped English move around the world.

Today, the ability to speak English is a requirement for about 750 million people around the world, and this population grows each year. In twelve nations, including the United States, Canada, Great Britain, and Australia, English is the native tongue of most people and the "official" language of government and society. In about forty more countries, including many African nations, English fluency is often necessary and sometimes useful, for it is the "semi-official" speech of those in leadership positions. Finally, from South America to East Asia, from Northern Europe to West Africa, instruction in English is given at all levels of education.

To be successful in almost any country today, one must speak English. Once an unimportant tribal speech, English is now used everywhere. In aviation, a Japanese pilot speaks to an Egyptian air controller in English. An Israeli or Korean scientist writes for publication in English. A German corporation and a Nigerian business in a joint venture decide to communicate in English to enable their workers to share a common tongue. World youth enliven rock and pop music by using English. And in the liberating movements in Southeast Asia and the democratic transitions in Eastern Europe, protestors speak to the world with banners written in English.

Two thousand years ago, the language you are studying was spoken by a small Germanic tribe in northern Europe. These people could neither read nor write, and the few words they had reflected their simple life. Even one thousand years ago, English was a minor language overshadowed in the West by French and Latin. But it was a language that grew, both in the size of its vocabulary and its influence around the world.

In the last one hundred years, however, qualities of the language combined with historical forces to create a powerful, important language studied and spoken throughout the world. To be understood in the world today, one must know English. In fact, this language may become a potent force to unify people into a global community.

## Questions

1. Return to the text and circle any underlined terms that you don't know. Try to analyze and form a literal definition for these terms by using the Glossary. If you still cannot form a clear definition, ask a member of your group to help you.
2. Write a short paragraph in which you give and explain several reasons why English has grown into an important world language. Read your paragraph to your group.
3. If English is not the native language of your country, explain its importance in your nation or culture. Read your response to your group.
4. If English is the native language of your country, explain how it continues to change and grow. Read your response to your group.

# II

# Prefixes

# 7 Negative Prefixes

The remaining units of this book are very different from those of *Part I*. In many ways, *Part I* was the hardest part of the text. While the affixes in *Part I* were related by grammar or function, the affixes and roots that you now will work with are connected by meaning. Additionally, in *Part I* you learned how to analyze and work with words. In the following units, you can begin to learn related words and quickly increase your vocabulary.

All the prefixes in this unit are negative prefixes, and you will see words you probably have never seen before. Here are a few suggestions that may help you through the unit:

**a.** Many of the words will describe something bad or unpleasant. You would not want people to use many of these words to describe you.

**b.** Many of the words are simply the opposite of the root or base word, and many of the words contain suffixes you have already learned; thus, you should be able to analyze many of them.

**c.** Almost all the words contain roots that are in the Glossary, so make good use of that section as you analyze words and give their literal definitions.

## WORD LIST

<u>a-</u> (<u>an-</u>): not, lacking, without

**Example:** **I had amnesia.** (state of lacking memory)

| | | |
|---|---|---|
| amnesia | amnesty | amorphous |
| anonymous | apathetic | atheist |
| atrophy | atypical | |

<u>anti-</u>: against, the opposite

**Example:** **Put antiseptic on the cut.** (against rotting)

| | | |
|---|---|---|
| antacid | antiseptic | antisocial |
| antitoxin | antonym | |

**dis-**: not, away, remove

**Example:**   **Class dismissed!** (sent away)

| | | |
|---|---|---|
| disagreeable | disconnect | disease |
| dishonest | disinfect | dismiss |
| distort | | |

**il-**: not

**Example:**   This writing is **illegible.** (not able to be read)

| | | |
|---|---|---|
| illegal | illegible | illegitimate |
| illimitable | illiterate | illogical |
| illusion | | |

**im-**: not

**Example:**   This fruit is **immature.** (not grown up or ripe)

| | | |
|---|---|---|
| immature | immeasurable | immense |
| immobile | immoral | immortal |
| immune | immutable | imperfect |
| impolite | | |

**in-**: not

**Example:**   The rules are **inflexible.** (not able to bend)

| | | |
|---|---|---|
| inaudible | incessant | incomplete |
| incongruous | inconsiderate | incorrect |
| incredible | incurable | infinite |
| inflexible | injustice | inoperable |
| insoluble | insomnia | intolerable |
| invisible | | |

**ir-**: not

**Example:**   Ice cream is **irresistible.** (not able to stand back from)

| | | |
|---|---|---|
| irrational | irrefutable | irregular |
| irreligious | irreparable | irrepressible |
| irresistible | irresponsible | irreversible |

mal-: poor, bad, evil

**Example:**     That is a **malicious** lie! (full of evil)

| | | |
|---|---|---|
| malady | malevolence | malfunction |
| malicious | malign | malignant |
| malnourished | malnutrition | malodorous |
| malpractice | | |

mis-: wrong, bad

**Example:**     I had a **mishap** this morning. (bad luck)

| | | |
|---|---|---|
| miserable | mishap | mislead |
| misplace | mispronounce | misread |
| misspell | mistrial | misuse |

non-: not

**Example:**     The judge is **nonpartisan.** (not on one side)

| | | |
|---|---|---|
| nonalcoholic | nonfiction | nonpartisan |
| nonprofit | nonresident | nonsense |
| nonsmoker | nonstop | |

ob- (op-): against, in the way, stopping

**Example:**     Our **opponents** were strong. (those who are against us)

| | | |
|---|---|---|
| obstacle | obstinate | obstruct |
| opponent | oppose | oppress |

un-: not

**Example:**     Treat **unequals** unequally. (not the same)

| | | |
|---|---|---|
| unbelievable | uncommon | unconscious |
| uncover | unending | unequal |
| unfinished | unfriendly | unhealthy |
| unkind | unlimited | unpleasant |
| unthinkable | untried | |

# Analysis

I.    Rewrite the following sentences, using the literal definition of the boldface terms in your change or revision. Your sentences may look very different from the ones given, but do keep the same meaning. The first one has been done for you.

1. I found their artwork **incredible**.

   *I could not believe their works of art.*

2. I cannot envision myself taking **illegal** drugs.

   _____

3. The city will not tolerate **malicious** acts.

   _____

4. We are frightened by **immense** and **incurable** diseases.

   _____

5. Your handwriting is **illegible**.

   _____

6. **Immature** behavior of older children sickens parents.

   _____

7. **Intolerable** heat does not pacify people in crowded cities.

   _____

8. This old house is **malodorous**.

   _____

9. **Apathetic** students rarely get good grades.

   _____

10. We must give you a shot of this **antitoxin**, or your life will be endangered.

    _____

II. Using the Glossary, analyze the boldface terms in the following sentences and write a literal definition that fits the sentence.

   1. He was always an **atheist**.

      _____

   2. After the accident, she suffered **amnesia**.

      _____

3. As he grew older, he became more **antisocial**.

   _____

4. Hot and cold are **antonyms**.

   _____

5. The class was **dismissed** at noon.

   _____

6. The mirror **distorted** my face.

   _____

7. The **illegitimate** child endured emotional pain.

   _____

8. Every nation has **illiterate** people.

   _____

9. Near the edge of the cliff, I stood **immobile** with fear.

   _____

10. Memorize the poet's **immortal** words.

    _____

11. Death is an **immutable** fact of life.

    _____

12. Air is **invisible**.

    _____

13. **Incorrect** answers minimize your chance of passing.

    _____

14. **Insoluble** problems enrage us.

    _____

15. Atheists are **irreligious**.

_____

16. The amnesia was **irreversible**.

_____

17. In poor countries, children suffer from **malnutrition**.

_____

18. Americans **misuse** drugs.

_____

19. What is the **obstacle** in our path?

_____

20. She had to pay **nonresident** fees at college.

_____

21. The judges were **nonpartisan**.

_____

22. Do you support or **oppose** the plan?

_____

23. I was **unconscious** after the blow to my head.

_____

24. Men and women are treated **unequally** around the world.

_____

# Relationships

I.  Most of the following terms are related to each other, but one does not logically fit.
    Cross out the unrelated term and give a category name to those remaining.

1. disease   malady   insomnia   malignant   miserable   misplace   malnourished

   Category: _____

2. unfinished   incomplete   imperfect   inaudible

   Category: _____

3. incomprehensible   unthinkable   illogical   irrational   unbelievable
   nonsensical   anonymous   incredible

   Category: _____

4. immeasurable   irreparable   illimitable   incessant   infinite   immense
   unending   unlimited

   Category: _____

5. impolite   unkind   disagreeable   unpleasant   inconsiderate   amorphous
   unfriendly

   Category: _____

II. Complete the following analogies, using words from the Word List.

   1. mispronounce : speak :: _____ : write

   2. _____ : phone :: cut off : electricity

   3. soap : clean :: _____ : disinfect

   4. government : _____ :: church : forgiveness

   5. guilt : accountable :: innocence : _____

   6. essay : _____ :: short story : fiction

   7. crooked : straight :: _____ : truthful

   8. grow : rot :: develop : _____

   9. _____ : stomach :: aspirin : head

   10. encourage : strengthen :: _____ : weaken

# Collaborative Work

The following sentences are hard to understand because they contain difficult words. In a group, discuss what each sentence means and then rewrite each in simpler English.

1.  An **inflexible, obstinate** belief in a **self-illusion** is not **atypical** human behavior.

    _____

    _____

2.  Righteous men and women often suffer **malevolence** when they **uncover** and try to rectify the **immoral injustices** of society.

    _____

    _____

3.  Given **immunity** from **malpractice**, the doctor used an **untried** way to destroy the **inoperable, malignant** tumor.

    _____

    _____

4.  If lawyers give **irrefutable** facts and avoid **incongruous** facts and **misleading** language, a **mistrial** is less likely to occur.

    _____

    _____

5.  Her laughter was **irrepressible**, her warmth **irresistible**, and her wisdom **uncommonly** deep.

    _____

    _____

# 8 Relational Prefixes I

Relational prefixes show how two objects or events are connected or related. In some ways, they are like prepositions, and the literal definitions of these words often contain prepositional phrases or verb phrases with prepositions. For example, we can say <u>under the water</u> or **submarine**, <u>across the sea</u> or **transoceanic**, <u>kick out</u> or **expel**. In these preceding literal definitions, **under**, **across**, and **out** are prepositions.

The prefixes in the Word List all show the position of an action or object, either in place or in time.

## WORD LIST

**ante-: before in time or place, in front of**

**Example:**      The **anteroom** is small. (a small room before a large one)

| | | |
|---|---|---|
| ancestor | ancient | antecedent |
| antedate | ante meridiem (A.M.) | anteroom |
| anticipate | antique | |

**pre-: before in time or place**

**Example:**      Look at this **prefix**. (placed before the root)

| | | |
|---|---|---|
| preamble | precede | precedent |
| pre-Columbian | precursor | predecessor |
| predict | prefabricate | prefix |
| pregnant | prehistoric | preindustrial |
| pre-law | premature | premeditate |
| premonition | prenatal | prenuptial |
| preposterous | preschool | prescience |
| preseason | presentiment | preshrunk |
| presort | preteen | pretest |
| preview | prewrite | |

post-: after in time or place

**Example:** The **postwar** recovery was slow. (after the war)

| | | |
|---|---|---|
| posterior | posterity | postgraduate |
| postindustrial | postmortem | postnatal |
| postpone | postscript | postwar |

inter-: between in time or place

**Example:** Send this **interlibrary** loan. (between libraries)

| | | |
|---|---|---|
| interactive | intercollegiate | intercourse |
| intercultural | interim | interject |
| interlibrary | intermingle | intermission |
| intermittent | intermix | international |
| interrupt | interscholastic | intersection |
| interstate | intertwine | intervene |
| interview | | |

# Analysis

Below are the literal definitions of terms from the Word List. Choose the word or phrase that best fits the sentence and definition.

1. "before the middle of the day": _____

   My first class is at 7:00 _____

2. "before in time": _____

   Airplanes _____ rockets.

3. "come before": _____

   Monday _____ Tuesday.

4. "look at before": _____

   _____ the chapter before you read it.

5. "something that happened before": _____

   The radio was the _____ of television.

6. "break between": _____

   Inconsiderate people _____ our talk.

7. "throw between": _____

   My brother _____ his immature comments.

8. "come between": _____

   The police officer _____ in the malicious argument.

9. "place after": _____

   The game was _____ because of intolerable heat.

10. "between countries": _____

    The _____ trade agreement was finally signed.


# Relationships

I. Arrange the following terms in the correct sequence, or the order in which they would logically or naturally occur.

   1. parents    ancestors    posterity    you

      _____

   2. intercourse    prenatal care    premature birth    pregnancy    postnatal care

      _____

      _____

   3. elementary games    preschool fun    interscholastic sports
      postgraduate study    intercollegiate athletics

      _____

      _____

   4. prehistoric tribes    postwar Japan    preindustrial Europe
      pre-Columbian America    postindustrial society    ancient China

      _____

      _____

II. Complete the following analogies, using words from the Word List.

1. front : anterior :: back : _____

2. conversation : letter :: afterthought : _____

3. halftime : sports :: _____ : theater

4. highway : state :: _____ : federal

5. _____ : talk :: application : write

6. _____ : compose :: revise : edit

7. interchange : freeway :: _____ : street

8. recall : past :: _____ : future

9. first : last :: _____ : final exam

10. old : new :: _____ : modern

III. One of the words in each group does not logically fit. Circle that term and name the category for the remaining terms.

1. prescience    premonition    presentiment    preamble    prediction    anticipate

   Category: _____

2. antecedent    precursor    precedent    preposterous    predecessor

   Category: _____

3. intermix    intermingle    interweave    intertwine    interim

   Category: _____

# Collaborative Work

In a group or with a partner, explain the following phrases and then use each phrase in a sentence.

1. prefabricated house _____

   _____

   _____

2. preshrunk jeans _____

_____

_____

3. presorted mail _____

_____

_____

4. pre-law student _____

_____

_____

5. preseason game _____

_____

_____

6. premeditated murder _____

_____

_____

7. intercultural communications _____

_____

_____

8. interlibrary loan _____

_____

_____

9. interactive computer _____

_____

_____

10. intermittent showers _____

_____

_____

11. postwar economy _____

_____

_____

12. interstate commerce _____

_____

_____

13. prenuptial agreement _____

_____

_____

14. postmortem exam _____

_____

_____

15. preteen clothing _____

_____

_____

# 9 Relational Prefixes II

The first set of relational prefixes (ante, pre, post, and inter) is used to describe connections that show before, after, and between. The next set is made up of those that show how people or objects may be higher, greater, and bigger or lower, lesser, and smaller than other people or objects.

## WORD LIST

sub- (sup-): down, under, lower

**Example:**    The temperature is **subnormal.** (below the typical)

| | | |
|---|---|---|
| subatomic | subcompact | subconscious |
| subdue | submarine | submit |
| subnormal | subscript | subsequent |
| substandard | substitute | subterranean |
| subtitle | suburb | subvert |
| subway | suppress | |

under-: down, lower, below

**Example:**    I am **undernourished.** (below the right amount of food)

| | | |
|---|---|---|
| underclass | undercurrent | underdeveloped |
| undergo | underground | undernourished |
| undersea | understudy | |

super-: higher, greater, larger, above

**Example:**    I sing **soprano.** (the highest voice)

| | | |
|---|---|---|
| soprano | superb | superhero |
| superhuman | superimpose | superior |
| superlative | supermarket | supernatural |
| superscript | supersonic | superstar |
| supertanker | supervise | |

<u>sur-</u>: higher, greater, larger, above

**Example:**     We can **surmount** the obstacle. (climb above)

| | | |
|---|---|---|
| insurmountable | surcharge | surmount |
| surpass | surplus | surreal |
| surrender | surtax | survey |
| survival | survive | |

<u>over-</u>: higher, greater, above, too much

**Example:**     We have a slight **overage**. (state of being over a limit)

| | | |
|---|---|---|
| overage | overcharge | overcome |
| overconfident | overcrowded | overdose |
| overeat | overlay | overpaid |
| overpass | overrun | oversee |
| overthrow | overturn | overview |
| overwork | | |

<u>out-</u>: higher, greater, better

**Example:**     I will **outlive** my parents. (live longer than)

| | | |
|---|---|---|
| outdo | outguess | outlive |
| outmatch | outnumber | outperform |
| outrace | outsmart | outthink |
| outwit | | |

# Analysis

I.     A few of the terms on the Word List are synonyms; in fact, the simpler synonym is actually the literal definition of the other term. From the Word List, choose the best synonym for each term listed below. Analyzing the given words first will help. The first one has been done for you.

1.  subterranean: <u>underground</u>

    Beneath the land was a **subterranean** river.

2.  supervise: _____

    I will **supervise** interlibrary loan activities.

3. superimpose: _____

Please **superimpose** the two charts.

4. surplus: _____

Do you predict a **surplus**?

5. surtax: _____

The government will postpone the **surtax**.

6. survive: _____

The children **survived** their parents.

7. submarine: _____

I did postgraduate work with **submarine** animals.

8. surmount: _____

We **surmounted** the postwar problems.

9. submit: _____

I anticipate that I will **submit** to the surgery.

10. survey: _____

The course is a **survey** of pre-Columbian history.

II. Analyze and provide a literal definition for each boldface term below. Substitute your literal definition into the sentence without changing its meaning.

1. Which of the two intercollegiate teams is **superior**?

_____

2. The antique plane cannot fly at **supersonic** speeds.

_____

3. Some international problems seem **insurmountable**.

_____

4. We have **surpassed** our goal.

_____

5. Preschool children cannot **suppress** their laughter.

_____

6. Our summer temperature was **subnormal**.

_____

7. The **overconfident** skier broke his leg on the steep slope.

_____

8. The **undernourished** child was intermittently ill.

_____

9. The swimmer was caught in an **undercurrent**.

_____

10. Women in our class **outnumber** men.

_____

# Relationships

I. Below are some related terms. For each set, write a sentence that explains how they are related or what they have in common.

1. superhuman          superstar          superhero

_____

2. super                superb          superlative

_____

3. subdue         subvert         suppress      overrun
   overthrow     undercut

_____

4. outdo           outmatch       outperform     outrace

_____

5. outfox          outwit          outthink      outguess

II.  Complete the following analogies, using words from the Word List.

1.  win : lose :: victory : _____

2.  initial : _____ :: leader : follower

3.  good : bad :: _____ : inferior

4.  math : _____ :: chemistry : subscript

5.  minimart : _____ :: boat : supertanker

6.  highway : bus :: tunnel : _____

7.  highway : _____ :: river : bridge

8.  _____ : actor :: substitute : athlete

9.  food : overeat :: drug : _____

10.  _____ : city :: electron : atom

# Collaborative Work

In groups or with a partner, answer the questions, do the problems, or simplify the sentences.

1.  What is the highest singing voice?

_____

2.  Describe a **surreal** dream.

_____

_____

3.  Name a compact and a **subcompact** car.  What is the difference?

_____

_____

4.  Where might you see **subtitles**?

_____

5. List two **supernatural** beings.

   _____

6. Name three **subatomic** particles.

   _____

7. When are you most aware of your **subconscious**?

   _____

8. Which sentence best describes you?

   _____  I'm underworked and overpaid.

   _____  I'm overworked and underpaid.

9. Rewrite the following sentence, using simpler English:

   Leaders of **underdeveloped** nations are wary about a permanent **underclass**, which endures **substandard**, **overcrowded** housing and whose **survival** is daily challenged.

   _____

   _____

   _____

   _____

   _____

# 10 Relational Prefixes III

With the exception of <u>counter-</u>, all the prefixes in this unit indicate a similarity or connection between two people, two objects, or two ideas.

## WORD LIST

**<u>co-</u>: with, together, joint**

**Example:** We must **cooperate**. (to make work together)

| | | |
|---|---|---|
| co-anchor | coauthor | cohabit |
| cohost | cooperate | cosign |

**<u>coll-</u>: with, together, joint; totally, completely**

**Example:** Two trains **collided**. (to smash together)

| | | |
|---|---|---|
| collaborate | collect | collide |
| collusion | | |

**<u>com-</u>: with, together, joint; totally, completely**

**Example:** I **combat** traffic everyday. (to fight with)

| | | |
|---|---|---|
| combat | combine | commence |
| commiserate | compare | compete |
| compile | compose | compress |

**<u>con-</u>: with, together, joint; totally, completely**

**Example:** When will this meeting **conclude**? (end completely)

| | | |
|---|---|---|
| concentric | concert | conclude |
| conduct | confer | confide |
| confirm | conflict | confront |
| congeal | congested | congregate |
| connect | consensus | conserve |
| consolidate | conspiracy | consult |
| contact | contract | convene |

**corr-**: with, together, joint; totally, completely

**Example:** You are **correct.** (completely right)

correct          corroborate          corrode
corrupt

---

**simil-** (**simul-**, **-semble**): same, alike

**Example:** Some couples **resemble** each other. (to look the same)

assemble          assimilate          resemble
similar           simile              simulcast
simultaneous

---

**sym-** (**syn-**): with, together, alike

**Example:** Are <u>hot</u> and <u>cold</u> **synonyms?** (having the same meaning)

symmetry          sympathize          symposium
synchronize       synonym             synthesize

---

**counter-** (**contra-**): against, opposite, back, response

**Example:** Do not **contradict** me. (to say the opposite)

contradict        contrast            controversy
counteract        counterargument     counterclockwise
counterexample    counterfeit         countermove
counteroffer      counterpart

# Analysis

Using the Glossary, give a literal definition for each of the boldface words.

1. _____ synchronize     Synchronize your watches.

2. _____ synonym         <u>Rock</u> and <u>stone</u> are synonyms.

3. _____ resemble        Children resemble parents.

4. _____ contradict      He contradicts me often.

5. _____ contrast        These are contrasting views.

6. _____ cohabit         We cohabited for two years.

7. _____ **compile**    I need to compile my notes.

8. _____ **combine**    Combine these stacks.

9. _____ **compare**    Compare these poems and choose the superior one.

10. _____ **correct**    Correct your mistakes.

11. _____ **collide**    The submarines collided.

12. _____ **collect**    Collect the money.

13. _____ **contact**    The metals were in contact.

14. _____ **convene**    When shall we convene?

15. _____ **conclude**    Part A is now concluded.

# Relationships

I.    Each of the following sentences contains two words from the Word List. If the words are synonyms (both words can be used in the sentence without changing the meaning), write "both" in the blank. If only one word makes sense, cross out the illogical term.

_____ 1.    We must (**collaborate/cooperate**) on this difficult project.

_____ 2.    This medicine should (**counteract/countermove**) the poison.

_____ 3.    The two superb armies were in (**combat/conflict**).

_____ 4.    I (**sympathize/commiserate**) with you; I, too, have failed a test.

_____ 5.    After work, the cars are (**corroded/congested**) on the freeways and overpasses.

_____ 6.    Those generals are in (**conspiracy/collusion**) to overthrow the government.

_____ 7.    I need to (**confer/consult**) with my supervisor.

_____ 8.    My story (**confirms/corroborates**) your story.

_____ 9.    The overconfident surgeon (**connected/compressed**) the torn muscle too quickly.

_____ 10.    Athletes (**confide in/compete with**) opponents.

II.   Complete the following analogies, using words from the Word List.

1.   cohost : talk show :: _____ : news program

2.   song : _____ :: poem : write

3.   _____ : concert :: coach : game

4.   agree : fight :: _____ : confront

5.   lie: speech :: _____ : money

6.   conclude : end :: _____ : begin

7.   politician : _____ :: fruit : rotten

8.   _____ : resources :: save : money

9.   lessen : grow :: _____ : expand

10.  loan : _____ :: book : coauthor

# Collaborative Work

With a partner or in groups, answer the following questions.

1.   What two types of weather tend to occur simultaneously?

_____

2.   Certain words are used to describe the change from one condition to another. Use each word below in a sentence that shows this change.

**EXAMPLE:**   _congeal_   _When I placed the sauce in the refrigerator,_

_it was silky smooth; in two days, however, it was com-_

_pletely congealed._ _____

a.   assimilate   _____

_____

b.   synthesize   _____

_____

**c.** assemble _____

_____

**d.** congregate _____

_____

**e.** consensus _____

_____

**f.** consolidate _____

_____

**g.** symposium _____

_____

3. Draw an object with perfect **symmetry**.

4. Draw a figure showing a **counterclockwise** motion.

5. Complete the following **simile:** I feel as heavy as a _____.

6. Name an object with **concentric** circles. _____

7.  Provide an example to each of the following **counter** words.

    a.  "All birds fly."

        Give a **counterexample**: _____.

    b.  "I'll give $600 for this car."

        Make a **counteroffer**: _____.

    c.  "Our Korean **counterparts** study much harder."

        Who are your Korean **counterparts**? _____

    d.  "Abortion is an immoral act."

        Give the **counterargument**: _____.

8.  Describe the most **controversial** topic at your school right now.

    _____

    _____

    _____

    _____

    _____

    _____

    _____

    _____

    _____

# 11 Prefixes of Movement I

The three previous units explored relationships or connections between ideas and items. Units 12 and 13 examine prefixes of movement. This unit covers prefixes of motion to, toward, into, through, throughout, and across something.

## WORD LIST

**ad-**: motion to, toward, into, next to

**Example:** **Adhere** to your values. (stick to something)

| | | |
|---|---|---|
| adapt | adhere | adhesive |
| adjacent | adjective | adjoin |
| adjust | admire | admonish |
| adverb | adverse | advise |

**ex-**: motion out of, out, outward, away from, beyond

**Example:** Some immigrants are **excluded.** (to close out)

| | | |
|---|---|---|
| examine | exceed | exchange |
| excite | exclaim | exclude |
| exhale | exhaust | exhilarate |
| exhort | expand | expel |
| expire | explain | explicate |
| explicit | explode | export |
| express | external | exterior |
| extract | extrasensory | |

**per-**: motion through, throughout; thoroughly, completely

**Example:** Fish odor **pervaded** the room. (to fill completely)

| | | |
|---|---|---|
| perennial | perforate | permanent |
| permeate | permit | perpetual |
| perplex | persistent | perspective |
| persuade | perturb | pervade |

pro-: motion forward, in front of, outward, upward

**Example:** What do you **propose?** (to put in front of something)

| | | |
|---|---|---|
| proceed | proclaim | procrastinate |
| procure | produce | prognosis |
| progress | prolong | promote |
| propel | propose | protagonist |
| protract | provoke | |

trans-: motion across, from one place to another, through

**Example:** I need to **transfer** buses. (to cross to another)

| | | |
|---|---|---|
| transatlantic | transcontinental | transcribe |
| transfer | transform | transfuse |
| transit | transition | transitory |
| translate | translucent | transmit |
| transparent | transplant | transpose |

# Analysis

Below are the literal definitions of some words from the Word List. Select the word that fits the meaning. You may need to change verbs to the past tense.

1. "push out; kick out": _____

   He was _____ from school for poor conduct.

2. "stick to": _____

   The tape will not _____ to a greasy surface.

3. "send through": _____

   No minors are _____ to enter the bar.

4. "move forward": _____

   After you compose the sentence, _____ to the next step.

5. "send across": _____

   The station _____ its signal from the huge tower.

6. "fit into": _____

   I sympathize, for I can't _____ to this cold either.

7. "through the years": _____

   Unemployment is a _____ problem.

8. "pull out": _____

   A dentist can _____ teeth.

9. "move forward": _____

   My supervisor will _____ me to co-anchor next week.

10. "carry across": _____

    I need to _____ money to my checking account.

11. "completely convince": _____

    My friends _____ me to stop smoking for my health.

12. "(look) to with wonder": _____

    I _____ the paintings of Rivera.

13. "shout out": _____

    "I won!" _____ the lucky man.

14. "shout forward": _____

    Nevertheless, the lucky woman was _____ the winner.

15. "change shape": _____

    College _____ his views on life.

16. "go beyond": _____

    If you _____ the speed limit, you might confront the police.

17. "turn to (bad)": _____

    In the _____ weather, cars collided all over the city.

18. "push forward": _____

    Paddles _____ a canoe.

19. "state of change": _____

   Compared to other changes, the _____ to college is often hard.

20. "move forward": _____

   We made some _____ last week toward settling the controversy.

# Relationships

I.  Write the opposite of each term. (The opposite will have the same root with a different prefix.)  Then write a sentence including both terms.

   1.  exclude / _____

       _____

   2.  exhale / _____

       _____

   3.  export / _____

       _____

   4.  explicit / _____

       _____

   5.  explode / _____

       _____

   6.  exterior / _____

       _____

   7.  external / _____

       _____

II. Each of the following sentences contains several words in parentheses. Read the sentence with each word separately.  If the sentence makes sense with a word, write "OK" above that word; if a word does not logically fit within the sentence, cross it out. (In some sentences, more than one of the choices will be acceptable.)

   1.  The smell of burning food (**pervaded/expanded/permeated**) the apartment.

2. Belief in a higher power has been a (**permanent/perpetual/persistent**) hope of humanity.

3. The president (**proposed/provoked/produced**) a new health-care plan that resembled the Canadian model.

4. The curtains in my room are (**transitory/translucent/transparent**).

5. My poor diet, lack of sleep, excessive work, and no medicine (**prolonged/protracted/procured**) my illness.

6. Algebra and calculus (**perturb/perplex/exhaust**) me.

7. My counselor (**exhorted/advised/admonished/persuaded**) me to take more English classes.

8. The cafeteria (**adjoins/adjusts/is adjacent to**) the bookstore.

9. Learning about other cultures (**excites/explains/exhilarates**) me.

10. In this course, students must (**express/examine/exchange**) their thoughts in collaboration with others.

III. Match the word from the <u>trans-</u> list to the object moved or changed.

1. _____ transcontinental     heart

2. _____ transatlantic     blood

3. _____ transplant     poetry

4. _____ transcribe     railroad

5. _____ transfuse     music

6. _____ translate     letters

7. _____ transpose     system

8. _____ transit     flight

Now use the matched pair in a logical, clear sentence.

1. _____

_____

2. _____

_____

3. _____

_____

4. _____

_____

5. _____

_____

6. _____

_____

7. _____

_____

8. _____

_____

# Collaborative Work

I.  In groups or with a partner, answer the following questions.  Try to use the literal definitions of the terms in your answers.

1. We say: "The time **expired** on the parking meter", "the patient **expired** at 4:00 P.M.", and "your license has **expired**." How are the three uses related?

_____

_____

_____

2. How do you **explicate** a poem?

_____

_____

3. What is the difference between an **adjective** and an **adverb**?

_____

_____

4. What is **adhesive** tape?

_____

_____

5. Describe or give an example of the following:

a. **extrasensory** perception

_____

b. a student who **procrastinates**

_____

c. a doctor's **prognosis**

_____

d. the **protagonist** in a play

_____

e. the **perspective** in a painting

_____

f. **perforated** paper

_____

II. English will sometimes borrow a word or phrase directly from another language with no change of the spelling. Here are a few phrases English has borrowed from Latin. What do they mean? You may need to use a good dictionary.

1. The speaker made a few <u>ad</u> <u>lib</u> comments.

_____

2.  We formed an <u>ad</u> <u>hoc</u> committee to study the problem.

    _____

3.  The speaker went on <u>ad</u> <u>infinitum</u> about Canada.

    _____

4.  The lawyer did <u>pro</u> <u>bono</u> work each week.

    _____

5.  The cost to you will be $100 <u>per</u> <u>annum</u>.

    _____

6.  Your <u>per</u> <u>diem</u> pay will be $75.

    _____

7.  The speaker went on <u>ad nauseum</u> about his political views.

    _____

8.  The <u>per capita</u> income of some oil-producing countries is very high.

    _____

9.  She made a <u>pro forma</u> apology.

    _____

10. The government increased the <u>ad valorum</u> tax on automobiles.

    _____

# 12 Prefixes of Movement II

The prefixes in this unit indicate a downward movement. Sometimes the downward movement is literal (as in **descend**), sometimes the movement is a breaking down or falling apart (as in **destroy**), and sometimes the lowering is more emotional or psychological (as in **demean** or **demented**). You will find that many of the words describe negative actions or harmful conditions.

## WORD LIST

**ab-**: motion away, away from, back

**Example:**     We **abhor** violence. (to be frightened away from)

| | | |
|---|---|---|
| abdicate | abduct | aberrant |
| abhor | abnormal | aborigine |
| abortion | abrade | abrupt |
| abstain | abuse | avert |

**de-**: motion down, downward, lower, to a lower level, away

**Example:**     The price **decreased**. (to move to a lower price level)

| | | |
|---|---|---|
| debate | decay | decelerate |
| decrease | deface | defeat |
| defective | defend | deficient |
| deflect | degrade | deject |
| delay | demean | demented |
| demolish | demote | denounce |
| depart | depend | deplete |
| deplore | deport | depose |
| depreciate | depress | deranged |
| descend | describe | desert |
| despondent | destroy | destruction |
| detain | deter | deteriorate |
| detour | detract | deviant |
| deviate | devour | |

# Analysis

Analyze and give a literal definition for the boldface terms. Use the Glossary.

1. Quick thinking by the diplomat **averted** a disaster.

   _____

2. When I fell from the bicycle, I **abraded** my knee and elbow.

   _____

3. Throughout the world, states and republics have **seceded** from larger unions.

   _____

4. Back home, my best friend and I were **inseparable**.

   _____

5. The hungry athletes **devoured** a huge dinner in ten minutes, and I waited for them to explode.

   _____

6. The lazy worker was **demoted** to assistant manager and transferred to Miami.

   _____

7. The business will **decentralize** its manufacturing process and move to Mexico to promote profits.

   _____

8. The world's oil supply is not permanent; it is slowly being **depleted**.

   _____

9. The goalie persistently **deflected** the shots.

   _____

10. We were **detained** at the customs office for three hours as they examined our bags.

    _____

11. I **abhor** the explicit violence on television.

    _____

12. The kidnapers **abducted** the child.

    _____

13. The city life **seduced** the young man.

    _____

14. We had a picnic in a **secluded** part of the park, adjacent to the pond.

    _____

15. The doctor advised him to **abstain** from alcohol for two years.

    _____

16. The movie came to an **abrupt** end, and the exhilarated audience cheered.

    _____

17. The gang **defaced** the subway walls.

    _____

18. The documents are **secure** in this box.

_____

19. The speaker **deviated** from her text to tell a personal story of her recovery from a prolonged illness.

_____

20. The constantly perturbed couple decided to **separate**.

_____

# Relationships

I.  In each of the sentences, give a literal definition for the boldface term (line **a**), and give a word with the same root that means the opposite of the boldfaced term (line **b**).

1.  The car **decelerated** on the ramp.

    a. _____    b. _____

2.  With a greater supply, prices should **decrease**.

    a. _____    b. _____

3.  The value of the auto **depreciated** during the year.

    a. _____    b. _____

4.  Tired and hungry, the hikers **descended** Mount Fuji and exchanged hugs.

    a. _____    b. _____

5.  The tire was **deflated**.

    a. _____    b. _____

6.  **Detach** the hose from the exterior faucet.

    a. _____    b. _____

7.  The **destruction** took only a minute, and the building was transformed to a pile of wire and concrete.

    a. _____    b. _____

8. The schools were racially **desegregated**.

   a. _____    b. _____

9. The odd sound permeated the auditorium and **detracted** me from my enjoyment of the concert.

   a. _____    b. _____

10. I am **deficient** in Japanese; I have trouble translating even easy stories.

   a. _____    b. _____

II. If you substitute the word in the second column for the original boldface term, which of the ten preceding sentences still make sense? If the second sentence makes sense, write a "yes" next to the sentence number below.

   1. _____   2. _____   3. _____   4. _____   5. _____

   6. _____   7. _____   8. _____   9. _____   10. _____

III. All the words in the following groups are related, except for one. Delete the illogical term and give a category name to those remaining.

   1. denounce   debate   defame   degrade   demean   deplore

   Category: _____

   2. decay   destroy   decompose   depend   degenerate   deteriorate   demolish

   Category: _____

   3. abnormal   aberrant   deviant   defective   demented   defeat   deranged

   Category: _____

   4. delay   detain   depart   deter   detour

   Category: _____

   5. abdicate   dethrone   depose   defend

   Category: _____

   6. depressed   describe   dejected   despondent

   Category: _____

# Collaborative Work

I.  Each of the following boldface terms indicates that something has been removed. Identify what has gone. Use the Glossary.

    1.  In the revolution, many people were **decapitated**. _____

    _____

    2.  The swarm of insects **defoliated** the trees. _____

    _____

    3.  The lost hiker was **dehydrated** and exhausted. _____

    _____

    4.  Promoted by advertisers, **deodorant** sales are on the rise. _____

    _____

    5.  Saudi Arabia has sought cheap ways to **desalinate** water. _____

    _____

    6.  The hurricane **depopulated** the island. _____

    _____

    _____

    7.  The border area was **demilitarized**, prolonging the peace. _____

    _____

II. What object might you . . .

    1.  debone: _____

    2.  declaw: _____

    3.  defang: _____

    4.  deice: _____

    5.  defog: _____

    6.  defrost: _____

7. dehorn: _____

8. decongest: _____

III. Answer the following questions or do the following problems. Use the meaning of the prefix in your answer.

1. What is an **abortion**?

_____

_____

2. Who are **aboriginal** people?

_____

_____

3. What is the difference between drug use and drug **abuse**?

_____

_____

_____

_____

4. Explain these two sentences:

a.  She **severed** her arm in the accident.

_____

_____

b.  The two nations **severed** all trade.

_____

_____

5. Why would a criminal be **deported**?

_____

_____

6.  What are the common **deciduous** trees in your native country?

    _____

    _____

7.  Rewrite the following sentence in simpler English by changing the boldface terms.

    The army could no longer **defend** the town, and it faced certain **defeat**. The forces **decamped** and many soldiers **deserted**.

    _____

    _____

    _____

    _____

# Review II

Give the meaning of the prefix; then analyze the boldfaced term and write its literal definition.

**Unit 7**  **Negative Prefixes**

| Prefix | Meaning | Phrase | Literal Definition |
|--------|---------|--------|---------------------|
| a- | _____ | an **atypical** day | _____ |
| anti- | _____ | stomach **antacid** | _____ |
| dis- | _____ | **disobey** the law | _____ |
| il- | _____ | **illegal** drugs | _____ |
| im- | _____ | **immoral** acts | _____ |
| in- | _____ | **insoluble** problem | _____ |
| ir- | _____ | **irregular** beat | _____ |
| mis- | _____ | **misspelled** word | _____ |
| mal- | _____ | **malignant** tumor | _____ |
| non- | _____ | **nontaxable** item | _____ |
| ob- | _____ | **obstruct** justice | _____ |
| un- | _____ | **unfinished** job | _____ |

**Unit 8**  **Relational Prefixes I**

| Prefix | Meaning | Phrase | Literal Definition |
|--------|---------|--------|---------------------|
| ante- | _____ | **antique** show | _____ |
| pre- | _____ | **preheat** the oven | _____ |
| post- | _____ | **postpone** the game | _____ |
| inter- | _____ | **interstate** highway | _____ |

## Unit 9    Relational Prefixes II

sub- _____    **subcompact** car _____

under- _____    permanent **underclass** _____

super- _____    Lake **Superior** _____

sur- _____    few **survivors** _____

over- _____    cost **overrun** _____

out- _____    **outlive** my parents _____

## Unit 10    Relational Prefixes III

co- _____    **cohost** the show _____

coll- _____    **collect** shells _____

com- _____    **compose** songs _____

con- _____    **congested** highway _____

corr- _____    **correct** response _____

simil- _____    **similar** problem _____

sym- _____    **sympathy** card _____

## Unit 11    Prefixes of Movement I

ad- _____    **adjacent** land _____

ex- _____    **expanding** waist _____

per- _____    **pervading** odor _____

pro- _____    poor **prognosis** _____

trans- _____    **transit** system _____

## Unit 12   Prefixes of Movement II

ab- _____   **abstain** from sex _____

de- _____   **detained** for hours _____

de- _____   **dehydrated** runner _____

se- _____   **secluded** spot _____

# Review II: Reading

The reading selection for Part II contains many underlined terms from the units. You should remember most of them. There are also several terms that are not in the word lists, but contain prefixes described in the units. Pay special attention to these terms by analyzing them, using the Glossary when you need it.

## The Harsh World of Gangs

In most major cities of the world, and American cities are no <u>exception</u>, gangs have become a serious problem. Once minor and almost <u>invisible</u>, these bands of young males, ranging from their <u>preteens</u> to mid-twenties, now <u>congregate</u> in groups of fifteen to thirty, looking for something to do. Often <u>unskilled</u>, perhaps <u>expelled</u> from school, these kids might simply "hang out," but sometimes this standing around leads to <u>explosive</u> fights and brawls; <u>conflicts</u> arise between urban gangs, and knives flash and guns fire. <u>Abruptly</u>, another young life is <u>destroyed</u>. The violence seems <u>nonsensical</u>, and the <u>antisocial</u>, <u>illegal</u> actions <u>perplex</u> us all. Many citizens <u>abhor</u> and <u>deplore</u> these <u>malicious</u> acts, yet they <u>persist</u>. Why? What <u>produces</u> such rage, such anger? Why do gangs seem a <u>permanent</u> part of urban life all over the world?

To <u>explain</u>, we need to know why a young man would join a gang, knowing his choice was both <u>irrevocable</u> and dangerous.

Why would a boy <u>submit</u> and <u>surrender</u> his youth to the physical <u>abuse</u>, <u>predictable</u> fights, and possible death that gangs offer? There are several powerful reasons.

The first is an escape from poverty. Most members have known <u>incessant</u>, <u>immutable</u> poverty. In gang neighborhoods, <u>unemployment</u> rates may <u>exceed</u> 40%, and what work exists is <u>demeaning</u>, <u>oppressive</u> labor with little future. Gangs, not <u>congested</u> schools or <u>miserable</u> jobs, seem to offer young men a break from poverty. Faced daily with <u>overcrowded</u> apartments or <u>substandard</u> housing, the youth seeks freedom in the streets.

In a gang, a young man finds <u>protection</u>, that is, a sense of belonging to a group. A gang is a kid's <u>substitute</u> family. A teenager who joins a group is taught to <u>defend</u> fellow members, and he is punished for <u>disobeying</u> the rules. Here is the acceptance and social <u>contact</u> that neither the <u>unhappy</u> home nor the <u>insensitive</u> school seems to offer. This is an <u>unhealthy</u> and <u>imperfect</u> family, yet the young man feels a belonging, a home.

And he may also be lured by an <u>incredible</u> sense of power. The power of a gun or rifle seems <u>unlimited</u>, for who will <u>oppose</u> a pointed weapon? And what he wants—cars, money, respect from his peers, sex, drugs— are the <u>irresistible</u>, <u>seductive</u> gifts the gang offers.

These reasons—the escape from poverty, the protection of belonging, and the lure of power—often <u>intertwine</u> to create <u>incredible</u> violence on city streets. To gain a gang's protection, a young man must first "prove" himself to fellow members by showing <u>disrespect</u> to other gangs or society in general. This means <u>provoking</u> a rival gang into a fight, <u>unlawfully</u> stealing cars, or even <u>illogically</u> shooting an <u>innocent</u> bystander at a downtown <u>intersection</u> in a crazy drive-by shooting. Once in the gang, a young man needs to maintain respect, power, and honor among his peers, and this often leads to even more <u>irrational</u> violence.

Still more violence arises when gangs <u>compete</u> for sales of <u>illicit</u> drugs. In large cities, each neighborhood is <u>controlled</u> by a gang; for another to sell drugs in the "hood" invites an <u>immediate</u> and <u>malicious</u> response. As gangs move their drug selling to other areas, the gangs in the smaller towns and <u>suburbs</u> are quickly <u>overrun</u> and <u>outsmarted</u> by the more violent ones from the city. And the <u>undercurrent</u> in this <u>disease</u> is an <u>amoral</u> <u>disregard</u> for much that most people everywhere value: law, decency, peace, and human life itself.

If society wants to <u>overcome</u> gangs and <u>deter</u> this violence, it must allow these young men to <u>surmount</u> poverty and <u>secure</u> power and protection in <u>nonviolent</u> ways. The gang <u>malady</u> is neither <u>incurable</u> nor <u>insoluble</u>. <u>Separately</u> and together, families, churches,

schools, and cities must <u>anticipate</u> the needs and <u>decrease</u> the <u>obstacles</u> in the way of these teenagers. But the greatest, almost <u>superhuman</u>, work falls to the young men themselves. They face <u>intolerable</u> problems they must <u>outmatch</u>, and they must find an inner strength to <u>transform</u> their lives. They have the biggest job, a <u>prolonged</u> battle that all of us must <u>support</u>.

## Questions

1. Return to the text and circle any underlined terms you don't know. Try to analyze and form a literal definition for these terms by using the Glossary. If you still cannot form a clear definition, have a member of your group help you.
2. Write a short paragraph about your experiences with gangs, either in your native country or the country you are living in now.
3. Look back to the word lists in Units 7–12. Using at least twenty words from the lists, write a short essay on one of the following topics:

   a. Manners and Etiquette

   b. Preparing for the Future

   c. Advertising

   d. Unemployment

   To do this, go back over the lists and write down all the words that relate to your topic. Then think of a main point you would like to make and write sentences that both support the point and include words from the lists. Read your short essay to your group.

# III

# Roots of Size and Study

# 13 Roots of Numbers

You have now learned the major prefixes and suffixes of English, so the rest of this book is devoted to the study of roots. In general, the root of a word is the base to which the affixes are attached. Most roots are not words by themselves; nevertheless, they carry very specific meanings. Knowing the meaning of the root of a word is a very important step in understanding the word.

The first roots are roots of number, and in each word the meaning of the root is consistent and regular. For example, almost every word containing the root <u>quad</u> will be in some way connected to the number four.

## WORD LIST

**semi**: one half

**Example:**     We have a **semiannual** sale. (every half year)

| | | |
|---|---|---|
| semiannual | semiarid | semicircle |
| semiconductor | semifinal | semimonthly |
| semipro | semiskilled | |

**uni** (**on**): one

**Example:**     I have twelve **units** here. (single parts)

| | | |
|---|---|---|
| lonely | once | unanimous |
| uniform | unify | union |
| unionize | unique | unison |
| unit | unite | |

**sol**: one, alone, by itself

**Example:**     The **sole** reason was money. (one, only)

| | | |
|---|---|---|
| consolidate | desolate | sole |
| solid | solidify | soliloquy |
| solitaire | solitary | solitude |
| solo | | |

mono: one

**Example:**  His voice was **monotone.** (one sound or tone)

| | | |
|---|---|---|
| monarch | monogamy | monograph |
| monologue | monopoly | monotone |

---

bi: two

**Example::**  I ride a **bicycle.** (two wheeled [vehicle])

| | | |
|---|---|---|
| biathlon | bicentennial | biceps |
| bicycle | biennial | bilingual |
| billion | binocular | bipartisan |
| biped | biweekly | combine |

---

du (di, do, twi): two

**Example:**  The tool has a **dual** purpose. (related to two)

| | | |
|---|---|---|
| dialogue | dichotomy | dilemma |
| divide | divorce | double |
| dual | duel | duet |
| duo | duplex | duplicate |
| twice | twilight | twin |

---

tri: three

**Example:**  The camera sits on the **tripod.** (three footed stand)

| | | |
|---|---|---|
| thrice | triangle | triathlon |
| triceps | tricycle | triennial |
| trillion | trimester | trinity |
| trio | triple | triplet |
| triplicate | tripod | |

---

quad (quar): four

**Example:**  There are four **quarts** here. (one-fourth of a gallon)

| | | |
|---|---|---|
| quadrangle | quadrant | quadrennial |
| quadriceps | quadrillion | quadruple |
| quadruplets | quadruplicate | quadriceps |
| quart | quarter | quartet |
| squad | square | |

**quin** or **pent**: five

**Example:** Draw a **pentagon.** (five angled figure)

| | | |
|---|---|---|
| pentagon | pentathlon | quindecennial |
| quintet | quintillion | quintuple |
| quintuplet | | |

---

**dec**: ten

**Example:** We begin a new **decade.** (ten year period)

| | | |
|---|---|---|
| decade | decagon | decapod |
| decathlon | decibel | deciliter |
| decimal | decimate | decimeter |
| dime | | |

---

**cent**: hundred

**Example:** My grandmother is a **centenarian.** (100 years old)

| | | |
|---|---|---|
| bicentennial | cent | centenarian |
| centigrade | centiliter | centimeter |
| centipede | centuplicate | century |
| percent | | |

---

**mill**: thousand

**Example:** We near a new **millennium.** (thousand year period)

| | | |
|---|---|---|
| mile | mill | millennium |
| millibar | milliliter | millimeter |
| million | millionaire | millipede |
| millisecond | | |

# Analysis

Analyze and give a literal definition for the following terms.

1. semifinal     The **semifinals** were held on Saturday.

_____

2. semicircle   The class sat in a **semicircle** and discussed aboriginal cultures.

_____

3.  lonely       "I wandered **lonely** as a cloud."—Wordsworth

    _____

4.  unify        The people **unified** against the monarch.

    _____

5.  uniform      Wages are not **uniform** in all nations.

    _____

6.  solitude     I enjoy the **solitude** of secluded forests.

    _____

7.  solidify     The water **solidified** into ice.

    _____

8.  monarch      Some nations still have a **monarch**.

    _____

9.  monograph    The **monograph** on early Chinese culture was deplored by the knowledgeable scholars.

    _____

10. monogamy     Most cultures practice **monogamy**.

    _____

11. bilingual    Millions of people are **bilingual**.

    _____

12. binocular    Most mammals have **binocular** vision.

    _____

13. combine      In math, we **combine** like terms.

    _____

14. dual         An eating fork has a **dual** purpose.

    _____

15. twilight     The inseparable couple walked each night in the **twilight**.

_____

16. tripod     The photographer set up her **tripod** on the Kenyan plain.

_____

17. tricycle     Kids fall off **tricycles**, abrading knees.

_____

18. decimal     Currency is often based on a **decimal** system.

_____

19. centigrade     In science, temperature is measured in **centigrade**.

_____

20. millibar     Air pressure is measured in **millibars**.

_____

# Relationships

I.    Arrange each of the following groups of words into a sequence that begins with the smallest and ends with the largest unit. Then identify the general category. Some of the words will not be on the Word List, so check their roots in the Glossary.

    1.   trio, quintet, solo, sextet, quartet, duet

_____

    Category: _____

    2.   centimeter, kilometer, decimeter, millimeter, meter

_____

    Category: _____

    3.   centipede, biped, millipede, octopus, decapod, quadruped

_____

    Category: _____

4. decade, quadrennial, triennial, quindecennial, millennium, biennial, century, millisecond, semiannual, biweekly, semimonthly, bicentennial, trimester

_____

_____

Category: _____

5. cent, quarter, dime, mill

_____

Category: _____

6. quadruplicate, centuplicate, duplicate, triplicate

_____

Category: _____

7. quintillion, million, trillion, billion, quadrillion

_____

Category: _____

8. double, quadruple, single, triple, quintuple

_____

Category: _____

9. triplets, quadruplets, twins, quintuplets

_____

Category: _____

10. triathlon, decathlon, biathlon, heptathlon, pentathlon

_____

Category: _____

II. In each sequence, one word is missing. Write a logical choice in the blank.

1. once, twice, _____

2. milliliter, _____, deciliter, liter

**93**

3. amateur, _____, professional

4. triangle, square, _____, decagon

5. biceps, triceps, _____

III. Complete the following analogies, using words from the Word List.

1. nurse's aide : _____ :: nurse : professional

2. monologue : comedy :: _____ : drama

3. majority : most :: _____ : all

4. _____ : marriage :: divide : divorce

5. _____ : strengthen :: disband : weaken

6. tropical : temperate :: _____ : desert

7. _____ : hundred :: per diem : day

8. gloves : boxing :: pistols : _____

9. _____ : harmony :: one : many

10. plentiful : common :: rare : _____

# Collaborative Work

Answer the following questions or do the following problems. You may need to consult a dictionary or other library resources.

1. Where would you find a **semiconductor** and what is its purpose?

   _____

2. How does a game of **solitaire** differ from other card games?

   _____

3. Why are **monopolies** illegal in many countries?

   _____

4. Describe a **monotone** speaker.

   _____

5. Describe a **bipartisan** committee.

   _____

6. How is a **dilemma** related to two?

   _____

7. Describe a person whose words and actions are a **dichotomy**.

   _____

8. Draw a **quadrangle** and divide it into **quadrants**.

9. Where would you expect to meet a **centenarian**?

   _____

10. What does a **decibel** measure?

    _____

11. How is a **mile** related to 1,000?

    _____

12. If a population is **decimated**, what exactly happens?

    _____

13. What is **solitary** confinement?

    _____

14. Why do schools **consolidate**?

    _____

15. Describe a **desolate** beach.

    _____

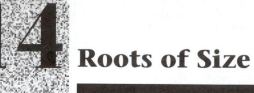

# Roots of Size

The roots and words in this unit are all related to size or amount, with a range from "nothing" to "little" to "full" to "huge."

## WORD LIST

**neg** (**null**): none, nothing

**Example:**    **The atom has one neutron.** (with no charge)

| | | |
|---|---|---|
| annihilate | annul | negate |
| negative | neglect | negligent |
| negligible | neuter | neutralize |
| neutron | nil | null |
| nullify | | |

**vac** (**van**, **void**): empty, leave, go away

**Example:**    **This room is vacant.** (empty)

| | | |
|---|---|---|
| avoid | devoid | evacuate |
| vacancy | vacant | vacate |
| vacation | vacuum | vanish |
| void | | |

**micro**: very small, unseen by the eye

**Example:**    **Use the microscope.** (instrument used to see small things)

| | | |
|---|---|---|
| microbe | microbicide | microchip |
| microcosm | micron | microorganisms |
| microphone | microprocessor | microscope |
| millimicron | | |

**min**: small, tiny

**Example:**  The car **diminished** in the distance. (grew smaller)

| | | |
|---|---|---|
| diminish | diminutive | mince |
| miniature | minimal | minimize |
| minimum | minor | minority |
| minuend | minus | minuscule |
| minute | | |

---

**brev** (**brid**): short, shorten

**Example:**  I use an **unabridged** dictionary. (not shortened)

| | | |
|---|---|---|
| abbreviation | abridge | abridgement |
| brevity | brief | unabridged |

---

**plen** (**plete**): fill, full, add to, finish

**Example:**  Oil is **depleting** rapidly. (opposite of fill)

| | | |
|---|---|---|
| complement | complete | deplete |
| plentiful | plenty | plethora |
| replenish | supplement | supply |

---

**multi**: many, much

**Example:**  **Multiply** these numbers. (increase many times)

| | | |
|---|---|---|
| multiethnic | multiflorous | multilateral |
| multimedia | multimillionaire | multiple |
| multiply | multistory | multitude |

---

**poly**: many, much

**Example:**  Draw a **polygon**. (many-angled object)

| | | |
|---|---|---|
| polyethnic | polygamy | polyglot |
| polygon | polygraph | polynomial |
| polynesia | polysyllabic | polytechnic |
| polytheism | | |

---

**omni**: all, everywhere, great, complete

**Example:**  Air is **omnipresent**. (present in all places)

| | | |
|---|---|---|
| omnipotent | omnipresent | omniscient |
| omnivorous | | |

**Example:** **Stress will magnify the problem. (to make larger)**

| | | |
|---|---|---|
| macroscopic | maestro | magistrate |
| magnanimous | magnate | magnificent |
| magnify | magnitude | majesty |
| major | majority | master |
| mayor | megabyte | megalopolis |
| megaphone | | |

# Analysis

Below are the literal definitions of some words on the Word List. Choose the word that matches the definition.

1. "to make into nothing": _____

   The penalty _____ the throw in the pentathlon.

2. "to make into nothing": _____

   The civil war _____ the peace efforts of the two previous decades.

3. "a small world or universe": _____

   A college is a _____ of society.

4. "To empty out": _____

   At the alarm, we _____ our duplex.

5. "the least amount": _____

   The _____ number of credits you must earn is thirty-six a year, or twelve a trimester.

6. "state of being short": _____

   Even a centenarian knows the _____ of life.

7. "the opposite of filled": _____

   Our combined supply of food is _____.

8. "to fill again": _____

   We must _____ our supply of food biweekly.

9. "one who eats everything": _____

   Bears are _____ quadrupeds.

10. "full of many flowers": _____

    Her garden has _____ roses.

11. "full of great spirit": _____

    The country was _____ with its help to the struggling nation.

12. "many mates": _____

    Some cultures practice _____.

13. "make larger": _____

    The centipede was _____ under the glass.

14. "related to many skills": _____

    She studied engineering at Virginia _____ Institute.

15. "state of being greater": _____

    The _____ of students in the bilingual class are Spanish-speaking sophomores.

16. "one that is nothing (sexually)": _____

    The animal is either female, male or _____.

17. "related to empty": _____

    The room is _____.

18. "many islands": _____

    The _____ islands are in the South Pacific.

19. "to leave (completely)": _____

    In the twilight, the robber _____.

20. "all knowing": _____

To young children, parents seem _____.

# Relationships

I.  Complete the following analogies, using words from the Word List.

1.  job : pay :: _____ : rest

2.  insecticide : bug :: _____ : germ

3.  penniless : beggar :: wealthy : _____

4.  _____ : city :: president : nation

5.  virus : _____ :: Saturn : telescope

6.  plus : minus :: positive : _____

7.  weak : mighty :: helpless : _____

8.  California : complete :: CA : _____

9.  bilingual : two :: _____ : many

10. second : _____ :: day : month

II. Use each of the word pairs in one sentence; then define the boldface word, using the meaning of the root in your definition.

1.  marriage/**annul**        _____

    _____

2.  set/**null**              _____

    _____

3.  motel/**vacancy**         _____

    _____

4.  pain/**devoid**           _____

    _____

5. onion/**mince** _____

_____

6. doll/**miniature** _____

_____

7. dictionary/**unabridged** _____

_____

8. vitamin/**supplement** _____

_____

9. treaty/**multilateral** _____

_____

10. expression/**polynomial** _____

_____

11. **polytheistic**/religion _____

_____

# Collaborative Work

I. In groups or with a partner, give a profession or field of study whose members would commonly use the following terms:

1. microchip    microprocessor    megabyte

_____

2. micron    millimicron    neutron    vacuum

_____

3. minority    multiethnic    megalopolis

_____

4. minuend    polygon    negative

_____

II. Read the following sentences and then answer the questions. Use the meaning of the root of the boldface term in your response.

1. The driver was arrested for **negligent** driving. The parents **neglected** their children.

   What did the driver do?

   _____

   What did the parents do?

   _____

2. This contract is **null** and **void**.

   What happened to the contract?

   _____

3. My savings are **nil**.
   My sister has **negligible** savings.
   My father has a **minimal** amount in his savings account.
   My mother has a **plethora** of savings.

   Financially, who is in the best and who is in the worst condition?

   _____

4. **Plenty** of **microbes** grew in the water. These **microorganisms diminished** when we purified the water.

   Give an example of a microbe or microorganism.

   _____

5. In college, I **majored** in business and **minored** in engineering.

   Explain the difference between a major and a minor.

   _____

6. The wine **complemented** the fish nicely. The colors **complemented** each other very well.

   How does one object complement another?

   _____

7. I didn't have time to read the novel, so I bought an **abridgement.**

   Describe what I bought.

   _____

8. The company presented a **multimedia** show to introduce its new computer.

   Describe the show.

   _____

9. I took the **polygraph** test at the police station.

   What did the police think I might have done?

   _____

10. The text was filled with **polysyllabic** words.

    Is **polysyllabic** a polysyllabic word? Why or why not?

    _____

11. He grabbed the **megaphone.**  She grabbed the **microphone.**

    Explain the similarity and difference between the two.

    _____

    _____

12. Define each boldfaced term. Then, explain what characteristic they all share.

    "Good evening, Your **Majesty.**"

    _____

    She was the chief **magistrate** of the city.

    _____

    He was a famous **magnate** of the nineteenth century.

    _____

    She was a chess **master.**

    _____

The **maestro** led the orchestra through the difficult piece.

_____

Shared characteristic: _____

_____

13. In each instance, what is being done to the problem or issue?

**annihilate** the problem

_____

**neutralize** the issue

_____

**avoid** the issue

_____

**minimize** the problem

_____

**complete** the problem

_____

**multiply** the problems

_____

14. Describe each of the following problems. Then, write a sentence with an example of the problem.

a **minuscule** problem

_____

_____

a **multitude** of problems

_____

_____

**omnipresent** problems

_____

_____

a **brief** problem

_____

_____

a problem of great **magnitude**

_____

_____

**multiple** problems

_____

_____

15. Where might I find **diminutive**, **multistory** buildings?

_____

_____

# 15 Roots of Location

Many English words describe how one object or idea stands in relation to another. Is it at the beginning or end of a process? Or is it in the middle, center, or around the outside of another object? The following roots and words reflect these locations and positions.

## WORD LIST

**prim** (**prin**, **pri**): first, most important, one

**Example:** We attended the **premiere** performance. (first)

| | | |
|---|---|---|
| premier | priorities | principal |
| prima donna | premiere | premium |
| primate | primary | prime minister |
| primer | prime | primitive |
| princess | primeval | principle |

**centr**: middle, in the middle

**Example:** We left **Central** Park. (related to the middle [of town])

| | | |
|---|---|---|
| central | centralize | centrifugal |
| centripetal | concentrate | concentric |
| decentralize | eccentric | egocentric |
| heliocentric | | |

**medi** (**meri**, **mid**): center, middle, halfway

**Example:** The show is **mediocre**. (halfway good and bad)

| | | |
|---|---|---|
| ante meridiem (a.m.) | intermediate | mean |
| median | mediate | medieval |
| mediocre | medium | meridian |
| midday | middle | midnight |
| remedial | | |

equi: middle, of the same value, identical

**Example:** I **equal**ed my best score. ([earned] an identical score)

| | | |
|---|---|---|
| adequate | equal | equality |
| equalize | equanimity | equation |
| equator | equilateral | equilibrium |
| equinox | equivalent | equivocate |
| inequity | | |

circul: around, round

**Example:** I **circul**ate at parties. (move around)

| | | |
|---|---|---|
| circle | circuit | circuitous |
| circulate | circulatory | circumcise |
| circumference | circumlocution | circumnavigate |
| circumspect | circumvent | encircle |

fin: end, complete, limit

**Example:** I **fin**ished the test. (ended)

| | | |
|---|---|---|
| *ad infinitum* | confine | define |
| definitive | final | finale |
| finish | finite | indefinite |
| infinite | refine | |

# Analysis

Analyze and give a literal definition for the following terms.

1. primitive      **Primitive** people were often polytheistic.

_____

2. primer      Our supply of **primer** will not cover the wall, but we have enough of the finish coat.

_____

3. heliocentric      Our solar system is **heliocentric**.

_____

4. concentric

Targets, onions, and logs all show **concentric** circles.

_____

5. mediate

To minimize the problems, the counselor **mediated** the argument between the divorcing couple.

_____

6. equalize

We **equalized** the pressure in the two tubes.

_____

7. equanimity

The president showed magnificent **equanimity** in the crises.

_____

8. equilibrium

The diminutive gymnast never lost her **equilibrium** during her floor exercise.

_____

9. circumnavigate

Magellan was the first European to **circumnavigate** the globe.

_____

10. circulate

Blood **circulates**. Books **circulate**.

_____

11. circuitous

We took a **circuitous** voyage through Polynesia.

_____

12. confine

The crook was **confined** to his minuscule cell.

_____

13. infinite

Numbers are **infinite**.

_____

14. define

Our rights are **defined** in our laws.

_____

15. refine

I completely revised and **refined** my speech.

_____

# Relationships

I. Complete the following analogies, using words from the Word List.

1. vice-president : president :: _____ : queen

2. human : _____ :: rat : rodent

3. average : best :: regular : _____

4. _____ : outward :: centripetal : inward

5. overture : start :: _____ : end

6. electricity : _____ :: water : plumbing

7. quadrangle : perimeter :: circle : _____

8. middle : median :: medium : _____

9. prime meridian : longitude :: _____ : latitude

10. _____ : heart :: digestive : stomach

II. Many of the words on the Word List cluster around certain topics. Explain each of the following phrases as it relates to the subject and use the meaning of the root in your explanation.

**Education**

**primary** grades _____

school **principal** _____

**final** exam _____

**intermediate** grades _____

**remedial** math _____

**middle** school _____

**Mathematics**

**prime** number _____

basic **principles** of calculus _____

**concentric** circle _____

**finite** set _____

the **mean** score _____

algebraic **equation** _____

**equilateral** triangle _____

**Time**

**primeval** forest _____

movie **premiere** _____

**prime**-time show _____

**midday** news _____

**midnight** meeting _____

a **middle**-aged man _____

the **Middle** Ages _____

**medieval** art _____

spring **equinox** _____

**ante meridiem (a.m.)** _____

**indefinite** hour _____

# Collaborative Work

I. In a group or with a partner, describe what someone means or what you must do if you hear the following. Then rewrite the sentence in simpler English.

1. "You must set your **priorities** in college."

   _____

2. "Stop acting like a **prima donna**."

   _____

3. "**Concentrate** on the instructions."

   _____

4. "I think your actions are **egocentric**."

   _____

5. "Your behavior has been quite **eccentric** lately."

   _____

6. "You cannot **equivocate** any longer."

   _____

7. "Please be **circumspect** with the prime minister."

   _____

8. "I think the question is completely clear, but all I get from you is **circumlocution.**"

   _____

9. "You always seem to **circumvent** the rules."

   _____

10. "All you seem to do is talk **ad infinitum.**"

   _____

II. Answer the following questions:

1. What country has a

   **premier?** _____

   **prime minister?** _____

   **prince/princess?** _____

2. How have **equal** opportunity programs tried to reduce social and economic **inequities?**

   _____

   _____

3. When and why are some males **circumcised?**

   _____

4. If you **encircle circles,** do you get **concentric** circles?

   _____

# 16 Roots of Measurement and Study

The roots and words in this unit are closely related to writing, studying, and measuring. Many are scientific or technical terms used to describe fields of study and instruments or tools employed in these fields.

Many new roots are introduced in the words, so you will need to use the Glossary.

## WORD LIST

**meter**: an instrument to measure something
**metry**: the measurement of something

**Examples:** The **barometer** fell. (tool to measure air pressure)

I saw an **optometrist**. (one who measures lenses)

| | | |
|---|---|---|
| altimeter | anemometer | barometer |
| diameter | geometry | metronome |
| micrometer | optometry | pedometer |
| perimeter | thermometer | voltmeter |

**graph**: an instrument to record something; write
**graphy**: the records or writings on a subject; study of

**Examples:** I read **seismographs**. (tools to measure earthquakes)

I read **biographies**. (life writings)

| | | |
|---|---|---|
| autobiography | bibliography | biography |
| cartography | choreography | demography |
| geography | graffiti | graph |
| graphite | monograph | oceanography |
| orthography | paragraph | photograph |
| seismograph | | |

olog: study of something

**Example:**     I like **geology.** (study of the earth)

| | | |
|---|---|---|
| anthropology | archeology | bacteriology |
| biology | cardiology | climatology |
| criminology | etymology | geology |
| meteorology | neurology | ornithology |
| pathology | pharmacology | physiology |
| psychology | sociology | technology |
| theology | zoology | |

gram: something written or drawn

**Example:**     Chinese uses **ideograms.** (written [characters] ideas)

| | | |
|---|---|---|
| cryptogram | diagram | grammar |
| ideogram | monogram | parallelogram |
| program | telegram | |

scrib (scrip): to write; something written

**Example:**     **Describe** your school. (write down [something])

| | | |
|---|---|---|
| circumscribe | conscripted | describe |
| inscription | manuscript | postscript |
| prescribe | proscribe | scribble |
| script | subscribe | subscript |
| superscript | transcribe | |

# Analysis

Analyze and give a literal definition for the following boldface terms.

1. Instead of medieval history, I decided to study **pharmacology**.

   _____

2. The **cardiologist** definitively told me I would need surgery.

   _____

3. I cannot **describe** the equanimity I felt during the crisis.

   _____

4. The **telegram** said they had reached the equator.

   _____

5. The Russian music was **transcribed** for guitar.

   _____

6. What **program** of study will you concentrate on?

   _____

7. In war, the army used the Navajo language for **cryptograms**.

   _____

8. The **inscription** began, "Give me your tired, your poor..."

   _____

9. The Central American quake registered 6.7 on the **seismograph**.

   _____

10. The essay contained six mediocre **paragraphs**.

   _____

# Relationships

I.  Circle the one word in the following groups that does not logically fit and write the general category to which the remaining words belong.

1. zoology    bacteriology    geology    biology

   Category: _____

2. pathology    neurology    physiology    theology

   Category: _____

3. ornithology    sociology    anthropology    criminology

   Category: _____

4. voltmeter    thermometer    barometer    anemometer

   Category: _____

5. manuscript   bibliography   choreography   monograph

Category: _____

6. grammar   orthography   etymology   parallelogram

Category: _____

7. oceanography   meteorology   climatology   technology

Category: _____

II. Choose a word from the Word List that logically fits the context of each sentence. (The word's root is in parentheses.)

1. The piano teacher reset the _____, and the student began to play. (meter)

2. The watchmaker measured the thickness of the gear with her _____. (meter)

3. Finishing his walk, the hiker glanced at the _____ that hung from his belt. (meter)

4. Everyone calls it lead, but the wooden pencil actually encircles _____. (graph)

5. The _____ on the subway and bathroom walls is rich in anger and eccentric humor. (graph)

6. I looked at the _____ at the end of the book for help with my research paper on primates. (graph)

7. The egocentric man had a _____ on each shirt pocket. (gram)

8. I add a _____ to all my letters. (scrib)

9. The actor studied the _____ before he accepted the role. (scrib)

10. The pilot glanced nervously at the falling _____. (meter)

# Collaborative Work

I. Below are some ideas or problems that are related to a field of study. Who would be interested in these topics? (You will need to change a word from the Word List to a "one who" word. For example, **biology** would become **biologist.**)

1. behavior, learning, mental illness   _____

2. ruins, artifacts, ancient cultures _____

3. eyes, glasses, lenses _____

4. light, shadows, cameras _____

5. maps, highways, rivers _____

6. population change, growth, statistics _____

7. clouds, snow, drought _____

8. sentences, adverbs, punctuation _____

9. currents, fish, pollution, tides _____

10. disease, virus, AIDS _____

II. Explain how the two boldface words are different __and__ similar in meaning. The differences will be easy to explain; the similarities may be difficult.

1. I studied the **diagram**. I studied the **ideogram**.

   _____

   _____

2. I am taking both **geometry** and **geography** this semester.

   _____

   _____

3. I cannot decide whether to read the **autobiography** or a **biography** of Malcolm X.

   _____

   _____

4. The **diameter** is shorter than the **perimeter**.

   _____

   _____

5. Math uses **superscripts** while chemistry uses **subscripts**.

   _____

   _____

III. Some of the <u>scribe</u> words are not directly connected to writing, but rather to written rules or guidelines. Based on the following boldfaced words, explain how these rules or guidelines work.

1. This gun-control law **circumscribes** my freedom.

   _____

2. My physician **prescribed** a muscle relaxant.

   _____

3. I cannot **subscribe** to the prince's ideas.

   _____

4. I was **conscripted** into the army.

   _____

5. The judge **proscribed** my behavior.

   _____

# Review III

Give the meaning of the roots; then analyze each boldfaced term and write its literal definition.

**Unit 13**  **Roots of Numbers**

| Root | Meaning | Phrase | Literal Definition |
|------|---------|--------|--------------------|
| semi | _____ | **semifinal** game | _____ |
| uni | _____ | **unique** person | _____ |
| sol | _____ | **solo** skater | _____ |
| mono | _____ | host **monarch** | _____ |
| bi | _____ | **bicycle** race | _____ |
| du | _____ | **dueling** skiers | _____ |
| tri | _____ | **triple** jump | _____ |
| quad | _____ | **quadrennial** games | _____ |
| pent | _____ | women's **pentathlon** | _____ |
| dec | _____ | last **decade** | _____ |
| cent | _____ | next **century** | _____ |
| mill | _____ | past **millennia** | _____ |

**Unit 14**  **Roots of Size**

| Root | Meaning | Phrase | Literal Definition |
|------|---------|--------|--------------------|
| null | _____ | **nullify** the gain | _____ |
| void | _____ | **avoid** the issue | _____ |
| micro | _____ | **microbe** hunters | _____ |
| min | _____ | **minimal** effort | _____ |

| brev | _____ | **brief** games | _____ |
| plen | _____ | vitamin **supplement** | _____ |
| multi | _____ | **multiple** events | _____ |
| poly | _____ | **polyglot** village | _____ |
| omni | _____ | **omnipresent** judges | _____ |
| mega | _____ | **majestic** setting | _____ |

## Unit 15    Roots of Location

| prim | _____ | **primary** reasons | _____ |
| centr | _____ | **eccentric** man | _____ |
| medi | _____ | **median** income | _____ |
| equi | _____ | lose **equilibrium** | _____ |
| circul | _____ | **circle** the globe | _____ |
| fin | _____ | the **finish** line | _____ |

## Unit 16    Roots of Measurement and Study

| meter | _____ | two meter **diameter** | _____ |
| graph | _____ | **geographic** study | _____ |
| ology | _____ | expert **neurologist** | _____ |
| gram | _____ | scary **telegram** | _____ |
| scrip | _____ | follow the **script** | _____ |

# Review III:   Reading

## The Olympic Games

The Olympic Games is a <u>unique</u> and <u>magnificent</u> sporting event that brings <u>multitudes</u> of the world's finest athletes together to compete, as the Olympic Oath says "for the glory of sport and the honor of our teams." <u>Millions</u> of spectators watch the games in person, and <u>billions</u> more follow the events on television. Held <u>quadrennially</u>, the summer games usually take place in a <u>major</u> world city such as Moscow, Seoul, Barcelona, or Atlanta, while the winter games are set <u>amid</u> <u>majestic</u> mountains, in winter resorts such as Sapporo, Calgary, Albertville, or Lillehammer.

The games always begin with the opening ceremonies. In summer, <u>uniformed</u> athletes from 160 nations, <u>encircled</u> by thousands of cheering spectators and hundreds of <u>photographers</u>, march proudly into a huge stadium. Once assembled, the com-

petitors are welcomed by the <u>prime</u> <u>minister</u>, president, or <u>monarch</u> of the host country, and then in <u>unison</u> the athletes recite the Olympic Oath. The Olympic flag, with its interlocking <u>multicolored</u> rings, is raised. <u>Finally</u>, in a dramatic moment a <u>solitary</u> runner carrying the Olympic torch <u>circles</u> the track and lights the Olympic flame, which burns brightly until all the events are <u>completed</u>.

And the games begin.

In winter, 1,200 men and women from sixty nations compete in seven events. <u>Solo</u> figure skaters spin and leap; dancing <u>duos</u> <u>complement</u> each other's moves as they glide across the ice. Speed skaters and bobsledders measure their swift races in <u>milliseconds</u> while skiers <u>duel</u> on the runs and jumps. And <u>biathletes</u>, in a curious sport, <u>combine</u> cross-country skiing and rifle shooting.

In summer, thousands of competitors vie for gold medals in well over fifty events, with the <u>premier</u> sports of swimming, track and field, and gymnastics getting the <u>central</u> attention of the world. The sights of these marvelous athletes in action is memorable: a huge weightlifter straining <u>biceps</u> and <u>quadriceps</u> to lift a thousand pounds; a <u>diminutive</u> gymnast keeping perfect equilibrium on the balance beam; a <u>sole</u> exhausted marathon runner exhorted by thousands at the finish line of a twenty-six-mile race; a finely muscled diver high above a tank <u>concentrating</u> with what seems complete <u>equanimity</u>; racehorse-like sprinters stretching their chests to cross the line <u>millimeters</u> ahead of rivals; <u>triple</u> jumpers who seem to hang in the air; overtired <u>pentathletes</u> pushing to <u>duplicate</u> world records; <u>quartets</u> of relay runners, streaming with sweat and wincing in pain, fighting to <u>equal</u> or exceed an Olympic mark; the tears of joy as the gold medal winners bow their heads to accept the precious prize.

And after the <u>final</u> medal is hung around the neck of the last victor, the ath-

letes reassemble for the moving <u>finale</u>, the closing ceremonies. This celebration, with beautifully <u>choreographed</u> dances and exploding fireworks, contrasts nicely with the formal beginning of the games. Athletes exchange uniforms, the Olympic flame <u>vanishes</u>, and the sights and sounds of another Olympics <u>unite</u> in memory as we recall the "swifter, higher, and stronger" athletes celebrated in the Games' motto.

Of course, not all the memories are pleasant, for the Olympics are not <u>devoid</u> of problems. Because the games are international, politics and conflicts affect them. Wars have canceled them five times in this <u>century</u>, and in recent <u>decades</u>, nations have <u>neglected</u> to send teams in order to make a political protest. And the problems have not been <u>confined</u> to mere protests: in 1972, terrorists <u>avoided</u> security and killed eleven Israeli athletes and a West German police officer in one of the ugliest moments of

Olympic history. Never had the ideals of the games been so <u>diminished</u>, so <u>negated</u>.

Despite the <u>negatives</u>, the games endure. In part, they persist because human beings glory in sport and competition, both the triumph and the struggle. And they will continue because for those few <u>brief</u> days, the world seems <u>unified</u> and the <u>polyglot</u> Olympic village becomes a <u>microcosm</u> of a world we hope to become, a world <u>solidified</u> by the <u>principles</u> of fair play and friendship among all peoples.

## Questions

1. Return to the text and circle any underlined terms that you don't know. Try to analyze and form a literal definition for these terms by using the Glossary. If you still cannot form a clear definition, have a member of your group help you.

2. In a paragraph or short essay, compare the most recent Olympics to the description given above. What did you notice that was similar, and what did you notice that was different?

3. Look back to the word lists in Units 13–16. Using at least fifteen words from the lists, write a short essay on one of the following topics:

   a. Communicable Diseases

   b. Exploration of the Earth

   c. Time

   d. Your School

To do this, go back over the lists and write down all the words that might relate to the topic you chose. Then think of a main point you would like to make and write sentences (using the words you listed) to support your point. Read your short essay to your group.

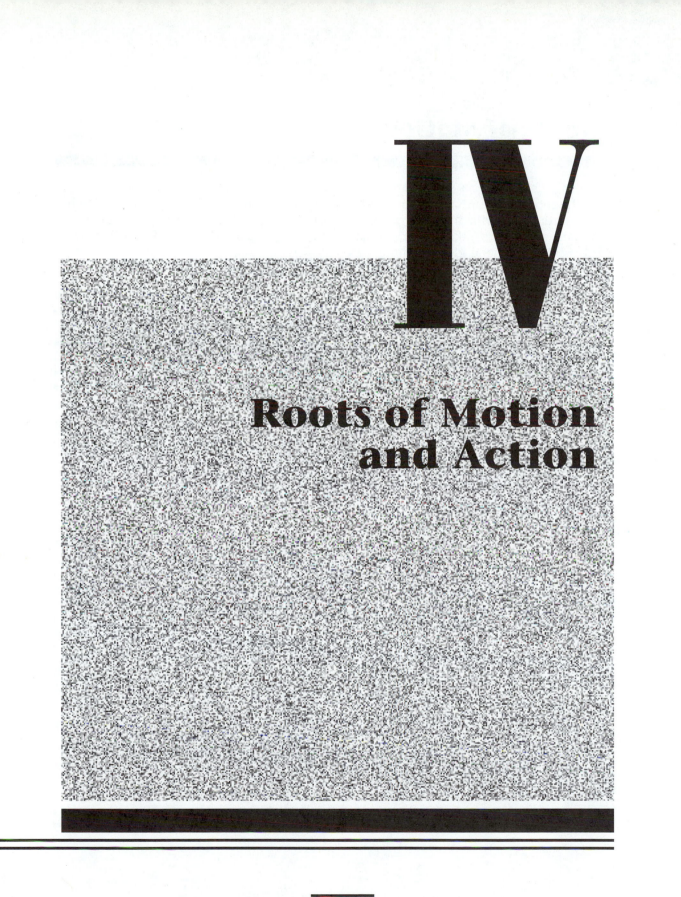

# IV

# Roots of Motion and Action

# 17 Roots of Motion I

The roots and words in Part IV are all connected to movement and action. English has many words to describe movement: go, flow, bend, push, pull, lead, and follow. There are also many actions: break, twist, carry, send, build, fold, kill, and die. Unit 17 contains words with the general idea of coming or going.

## WORD LIST

cycle: wheel, circle

**Example:** I have two **bicycles.** (two-wheeled vehicle)

| | | |
|---|---|---|
| bicycle | cycle | cyclical |
| cycling | cyclone | cyclotron |
| encyclopedia | motorcycle | |

mob (mot, mov): to move

**Example:** I was **immobilized.** (not able to move)

| | | |
|---|---|---|
| automobile | commotion | demote |
| electromotive | immobilize | mob |
| mobility | momentum | motel |
| motile | motion | motionless |
| motivate | motive | movie |
| promote | | |

cede (cess, ceed): to go; stop, give up

**Example:** We have had **incessant** rain. (without a stop)

| | | |
|---|---|---|
| ancestor | antecedent | cease |
| concede | deceased | exceed |
| inaccessible | incessant | intercede |
| precede | precedent | predecessor |
| proceed | recede | secede |
| succeed | | |

> **ven**: to come, come about, happen, occur
>
> **Example:**    We waited for the final **event.** (something that happens)
>
> | | | |
> |---|---|---|
> | advent | avenue | circumvent |
> | convene | event | intervene |
> | invent | prevent | revenue |
> | venture | venue | |

# Analysis

Choose a word from the Word List to match the literal definition and the context of the sentence.

1. "move forward": _____

   The cartographer was _____ to a new job.

2. "come together": _____

   The Technology Committee will _____ at 8:00 a.m. tomorrow.

3. "go beyond": _____

   My expenses _____ my income.

4. "related to circles": _____

   The seasons are _____.

5. "not able to move": _____

   He stood on the diving board, _____ with fear.

6. "move down": _____

   The pathologist was _____ to his old job.

7. "not able to go to": _____

   The top of the mountain was _____ to the biologist.

8. "go before": _____

   July _____ September.

9. "go forward": _____

   _____ to the next set of grammar exercises.

10. "come between": _____

    The police _____ in the fight.

11. "to make move": _____

    Pride, money, and love _____ many people to accomplish great
    goals.

12. "go after": _____

    President Clinton _____ President Bush.

13. "go back": _____

    The tide began to _____ at midnight.

14. "complete movement": _____

    The room was full of _____.

15. "go away": _____

    The Republics _____ from the Union.

# Relationships

I.   Complete the following analogies, using words from the Word List.

   1. _____ : child :: motorcycle : adult

   2. dictionary : words :: _____ : "circle" of all
      knowledge

   3. plants : sessile :: animals : _____

   4. inertia : _____ :: sit : move

   5. intermittent : interrupted :: _____ : continuous

   6. path : trail :: _____ : street

   7. discover : _____ :: find : create

8. _____ : wind :: eddy : water

9. surrender : general :: _____ : candidate

10. _____ : parent :: you : your children

II. Create a logical, clear sentence for each of the following word pairs. Then rewrite your sentences in simpler English.

1. cease/mobility

_____

_____

2. mob/prevent

_____

_____

3. deceased/motionless

_____

_____

4. motive/venture

_____

_____

5. circumvent/revenue

_____

_____

# Collaborative Work

I.   Certain words on the Word List are often used in specialized fields. Explain in simple English what the underlined words or phrases mean in the given fields.

## Law

1.   The lawyer will <u>intercede on your behalf</u> with the judge.

   _____

2.   The lawyer will <u>look for a precedent</u> in your case.

   _____

3.   If there is too much publicity, your lawyer will ask for a <u>change of venue</u>.

   _____

## Physics

1.   <u>An object in motion</u> tends to stay in motion.

   _____

2.   Batteries are simple <u>electromotive devices</u>.

   _____

3.   The atomic scientists examined the <u>cyclotron</u>.

   _____

## Recreation

1.   People of all ages enjoy <u>cycling</u>.

   _____

2.   Each night, we stayed in a different <u>motel</u>.

   _____

3.   Each night, we saw a new <u>movie</u>.

   _____

II.   List at least ten forms of transportation (from the Word List and from your own knowledge) that have <u>cycle</u> or <u>mot</u> as their root.

1.   _____

2.   _____

3.   _____

4.   _____

5.   _____

6.   _____

7.   _____

8.   _____

9.   _____

10.   _____

# 18 Roots of Motion II

The words in this unit again deal with general motion, but you will notice that most of the words refer to forward movement.

## WORD LIST

cur (cour): to flow, run, happen

**Example:** The **current** is swift. (flow of [water])

| | | |
|---|---|---|
| concourse | concur | concurrent |
| corridor | courier | course |
| current | cursive | cursor |
| cursory | excursion | incur |
| precursor | recur | |

flu (flo): to flow, to float

**Example:** Prices **fluctuate**. (flow [up and down])

| | | |
|---|---|---|
| affluent | confluence | effluent |
| fleet | floe | flood |
| flotilla | flotsam | fluctuate |
| flue | fluent | fluid |
| flume | flush | mellifluous |

duc: to lead, guide, carry

**Example:** College **introduces** you to much. (leads into)

| | | |
|---|---|---|
| abduct | aqueduct | conducive |
| conduct | conduit | deduct |
| docile | duct | ductile |
| duke | induce | introduce |
| produce | reduce | reproduce |
| seduce | viaduct | |

sequ (sec, sue): to follow, come after

**Example:**   A fight **ensued.** (followed after)

| | | |
|---|---|---|
| consecutive | consequently | ensue |
| non sequitur | obsequious | persecute |
| prosecute | pursue | sect |
| sequel | sequence | subsequent |

grad (gress): to move, go step by step, come

**Example:**   We made **progress.** (a movement forward)

| | | |
|---|---|---|
| aggression | congress | degrade |
| degree | digress | grade |
| gradient | gradual | graduate |
| progress | regress | transgress |

# Analysis

Analyze the following terms. Then, rewrite the sentence using your literal definitions.

1. recur      Cyclical problems _____ .

     _____

2. concurrent      There were three _____ meetings.

     _____

3. effluent      The polluted _____ from the factory exceeded federal standards.

     _____

     _____

4. gradual      My recovery from the flu was _____ .

     _____

5. digress     The speaker felt motivated to _____ from her topic to tell a personal story.

_____

_____

6. <u>non sequitur</u>    What you say is a _____ .

_____

7. conducted    She _____ the orchestra flawlessly.

_____

8. reduce    Exercise and diet will _____ your weight to normal.

_____

_____

9. precursor    The carriage was a _____ to the automobile.

_____

10. concur    Our opinions _____ .

_____

# Relationships

I.    Complete the following analogies, using words from the Word List.

1. graceful : dancer :: _____ : speaker

2. reservoir : storage :: _____ : movement

3. _____ : electricity :: flow : water

4. corridor : school :: _____ : airport

5. wood : water :: solid : _____

6. _____ : original :: *Son of Frankenstein* : *Frankenstein*

7. retire : _____ :: job : school

8. legislature : state :: _____ : nation

9. progress : forward :: _____ : backward

10. rivers : _____ :: streets : intersections

11. squadron : planes :: _____ : ships

12. rank : _____ :: military : school

13. _____ : child :: steal : car

14. princess : prince :: duchess : _____

15. unbroken : interrupted :: _____ : irregular

II. Many of the terms on the Word List have more than one meaning. Explain all of the following uses of the word in terms of the root.

1. I will study the bicycle race **course**.

   _____

   I will study the **course** of the disease.

   _____

2. The runners were **fleet**.

   _____

   The **fleet** sailed into the Persian Gulf.

   _____

3. I **flushed** the toilet.

   _____

   My face was **flushed** after the triathlon.

   _____

4. My basement **flooded** every spring.

   _____

   My mailbox was **flooded** with junk mail.

   _____

5. The thermometer rose two **degrees** every hour.

_____

He was immobilized by a third-**degree** burn.

_____

I earned my **degree** after four years of incessant study.

_____

6. The currency was **degraded**.

_____

I felt **degraded** by your rude comment.

_____

7. The electric wires were enclosed in a **conduit**.

_____

Miami is a major **conduit** of drugs into the United States.

_____

8. The death of my uncle **induced** me to stop smoking.

_____

The drug **induced** labor, and the child was soon born.

_____

9. The heating **duct** was blocked.

_____

My tear **duct** was blocked.

_____

10. She **produced** and promoted the movie.

_____

That factory **produces** a car every two minutes.

_____

Long, important tests **produce** anxiety in students.

_____


# Collaborative Work

I.    Rewrite the following sentences into simpler English. Try to use the meaning of the roots in your new sentences and compare your "product" with those of others in your group. Then, either choose the best revision or create a better one from the ones your group has written.

1. **Subsequent** to its feeding, the lion became **docile**.

    _____

    _____

2. **Affluent** people never cease watching the **fluctuations** of stock prices.

    _____

    _____

3. The **courier** had a bicycle accident on the **viaduct**.

    _____

    _____

4. I was **introduced** to moral **transgression** at a young age.

    _____

    _____

5. Urban living is **conducive** to **aggression**.

    _____

    _____

6. Copper is **ductile; consequently**, it is used in wires.

_____

_____

7. If you are always **obsequious** to your boss, you may **incur** the anger of coworkers.

_____

_____

_____

8. Members of religious **sects** often feel they are **persecuted**.

_____

_____

9. To **pursue** a major in business, I need to take the accounting **sequence**.

_____

_____

10. On our **excursion** into the forest, we heard the **mellifluous** sound of a small stream bubbling over the rocks.

_____

_____

_____

II.  Answer the following questions, using the meaning of a root in your answer.

1. What is **cursive** writing?

_____

2. With a **cursory** reading of a text, can you hope to get a good grade?

_____

3. Why is a computer's **cursor** so named?

_____

4.   What will **ensue** if your employer fails to **deduct** income tax from your paycheck?

_____

5.   Where might you find:

a floe? _____

a flume? _____

flotsam? _____

a flue? _____

a concourse? _____

a corridor? _____

a current? _____

a courier? _____

a flotilla? _____

a duke? _____

an aqueduct? _____

a conduit? _____

a duct? _____

a viaduct? _____

# 19 Roots of Motion III

Movements are frequently caused or forced. There is an agent (the mover) and the object (whatever is moved). These movements are sometimes small and slight. Such movements, involving stretching, tightening, pressing, and joining, are introduced in this unit.

## WORD LIST

**tend** (**tens**, **tent**): to stretch, move, be tight, be pulled

**Example:**  **Extend** the hours. (stretch them out)

| | | |
|---|---|---|
| attend | attenuate | contend |
| distend | extend | extensive |
| intensify | intensive | tendency |
| tendon | tense | tensile |
| tension | tent | |

**strict** (**stren**, **strin**, **strain**, **stress**): to tighten, be tight; in a straight line because pulled

**Example:**  Our muscles **constrict**. (tighten together)

| | | |
|---|---|---|
| astringent | constrict | distress |
| restrain | straight | strain |
| strait | strangle | stray |
| streak | street | strenuous |
| stressful | stretch | strict |
| stringent | unrestricted | |

**junc** (**joi**): to blend, unite, put together

**Example:**  We met at the **junction**. (a place where roads join)

| | | |
|---|---|---|
| adjoin | adjunct | conjoin |
| conjugal | conjunction | disjoin |
| enjoin | join | joint |
| junction | juncture | yoke |

# Analysis

Choose a word from the Word List to match the literal definitions.

1. "push back": _____

   I could not _____ my laughter.

   He _____ the unpleasant memory of persecution.

2. "not joined": _____

   His ensuing speech was _____.

   _____ the chicken before cooking.

3. "stretch out": _____

   I will _____ my hand to you.

   We induced the instructor to _____ the due date.

4. "tighten together": _____

   Our muscles _____ and relax.

   The snake _____ its prey before it ate it.

5. "stretch outward": _____

   The stomachs of starving children _____.

   His appendix gradually _____ and then burst.

6. "join together": _____

   The two armies _____ their forces.

   Men and women, _____ with a common purpose, marched in protest of the government's new law.

7. "push together": _____

   We can _____ gases, but not liquids.

   The time seemed _____.

8. "join to": _____

   The lab _____ the classroom.

   All the offices in this corridor are _____.

9. "push down": _____

   Slaves are _____ people.

   _____ people will often aggressively rise up.

10. "state of being tight": _____

    _____ filled my body.

    _____ rose as the market began to fluctuate wildly.

11. "related to tight": _____

    I live on a _____ budget.

    There is a _____ sequence of steps to follow.

12. "state of being pulled": _____

    Fight the _____ to sleep.

    Affluent people have a _____ to forget the poor.

13. "full of tightness": _____

    A student's life is _____.

    Progress can produce _____ change.

14. "state of joining": _____

    Check the fuse at the _____ box.

    The stadium is at the confluence of the rivers and the _____ of the interstates.

15. "push out": _____

    I cannot _____ how happy I feel.

    He seems to _____ himself in <u>non sequiturs</u>.

16. "to be pulled toward": _____

    I cannot _____ class today.

    I must _____ to my studies this week.

17. "fight together": _____

    All students _____ with lines.

    The boxers will _____ for the world heavyweight title.

18. "state of being joined": _____

    At this _____ of my life, between old age and death, I feel at peace.

    At this _____, we need to take a break.

# Relationships

When an object is stretched, it may become tight, straight, or strong. Determine for each of the following words how the term is related to straightness, tightness, or strength.

1. I feel **tense**.

   _____

2. The competition **intensified**.

   _____

3. My muscles **strained**.

   _____

141

4. I walked down the **street**.

   _____

5. I rubbed the **astringent** on my sore.

   _____

6. The ship entered the **Straits** of Gibraltar.

   _____

7. Put up the **tent** next to that tree.

   _____

8. He wanted to **strangle** his brother.

   _____

9. The comet **streaked** across the sky.

   _____

10. The collar **restrained** the dog.

    _____

11. Her rules were **strict**.

    _____

12. I enjoy **strenuous** exercise.

    _____

13. I was **distressed** by the bad news.

    _____

14. Your **tendon** is damaged.

    _____

15. His problem **attenuated** slowly.

    _____

# Collaborative Work

Answer the following questions. Use the meaning of the root in your answer.

1. Who has **conjugal** visits?

   _____

2. Who are **adjunct** faculty?

   _____

3. What is the purpose of a **conjunction** in a sentence?

   _____

4. What do **joints** in your body join?

   _____

5. What does a **yoke** join?

   _____

6. What is an appetite **suppressant**?

   _____

7. What is a tongue **depressor**?

   _____

8. What are the greatest **pressures** in a student's life?

   _____

9. What is an **impressionable** youth?

   _____

10. What is an **irrepressible** laugh?

    _____

11. What is the difference between "**intensive** reading" and "**extensive** reading"?

    _____

12. What is the **tensile** strength of a wire?

    _____

# 20 Roots of Motion IV

Breaking, twisting, turning, and bending are the movements described by the roots and words in this unit. Many of the words are negative; a large number are connected to pain and suffering.

## WORD LIST

**fract (frag, fring): to break, be broken**

**Example:** The vase is **fragile.** (easily broken)

| | | |
|---|---|---|
| diffract | fraction | fracture |
| fragile | fragment | frail |
| frangible | infraction | infringe |
| refract | | |

**rupt: to break, burst, burst out**

**Example:** I gave an **abrupt** answer. (break off suddenly)

| | | |
|---|---|---|
| abrupt | bankrupt | disrupt |
| erupt | incorruptible | interrupt |
| rupture | | |

**tort: to twist**

**Example:** This river is **tortuous.** (full of twists)

| | | |
|---|---|---|
| contort | distort | extort |
| nasturtium | tart | torque |
| torso | tortuous | torture |

144

vert (vers): to turn, change

**Example:**  I **reverted** to my earlier method. (changed back)

| | | |
|---|---|---|
| adverse | anniversary | avert |
| controversy | conversation | converse |
| convert | diversions | divert |
| introvert | invert | pervert |
| revert | versatile | version |
| vertebrae | vertigo | |

flect (flex): to bend, move in the opposite direction, change

**Example:**  My teachers seem **flexible**.  (able to bend or change)

| | | |
|---|---|---|
| deflect | flex | flexible |
| flexor | flextime | genuflect |
| inflexible | reflect | reflective |
| reflex | | |

# Analysis

Analyze the following terms and write a literal definition for each one.

1.  flexible: _____

    The plumber compressed the **flexible** tubing.

2.  convert: _____

    We have **converted** to the metric system.

3.  distort: _____

    The mirror **distorted** my face.

4.  erupt: _____

    For three consecutive years, the volcano **erupted** in impressive smoke, fire, and ash.

5.  fragment: _____

    **Fragments** of rock blew out of the eruption.

6. reflect: _____

   Your face **reflects** your strain and stress.

7. revert: _____

   Even adults may **revert** to docile, childlike behavior.

8. tortuous: _____

   Drivers on the mountain contended with **tortuous** curves.

9. interrupt: _____

   The recurrent ringing phone in the adjoining office **interrupted** our conversation.

10. fracture: _____

    The **fracture** will slowly heal, but the joint will not.

11. extort: _____

    The crime boss **extorted** money from the affluent businessman.

12. pervert: _____

    Gradually, the original ideals of the country were **perverted**, and oppression grew.

13. deflect: _____

    The boxer neatly **deflected** the strenuous blows.

14. avert: _____

    In shyness, I **averted** my eyes from my classmates and suppressed my desire to talk.

15. infringe: _____

    Smokers sometimes **infringe** upon the rights of nonsmokers.

# Relationships

I.  Many of the words on the Word List relate to the functions and problems of our bodies. Explain the following phrases in terms of the human body; try to use the meaning of the root in your explanation.

1. a **fragile** bone

   _____

2. a **frail** old man

   _____

3. a **ruptured** kidney

   _____

4. a slender **torso**

   _____

5. two broken **vertebrae**

   _____

6. intense **vertigo**

   _____

7. an **inflexible** elbow

   _____

8. **flex** my muscles

   _____

9. the **reflex** in my knee

   _____

10. **genuflect** at the altar

    _____

11. tensors and **flexors** of the leg

    _____

II. In each set of sentences, the first one contains a phrase that is a clue to the missing word in the second one. Choose a word from the Word List that logically completes the sentence.

   1. The peace talks were suddenly broken off.  Both sides seemed surprised at the

      _____ end.

2. You have broken the law again. Because of your extensive list of _____, you will need to pay a $200 fine.

3. We have financial distress; we are broke. We will become _____.

4. If they break into shouts again, we will stop the meeting. They should not be allowed to _____ us anymore.

5. You have twisted my arm cruelly. I don't think I can bear the distress of such _____.

6. Look at his twisted face! The apple he is eating must be _____.

7. Look at those wrestlers twisted together. I'm incredulous at how they can _____ their bodies in such strange ways.

8. He turns inward often when he is around people. No wonder everyone calls him an _____.

9. As another year turns, we celebrate one more _____ of conjugal happiness.

10. Now your turn to talk has come. Could you express your _____ of the story to the prosecutor?

11. People have turned against each other on the abortion issue. People will never join hands on such a _____.

12. The weather has taken a turn to the worse. I cannot drive in these _____ conditions.

13. If we turn this flood away, we might save the house. Do we have enough time to _____ the water?

14. You can turn this tool into a hammer, pliers, wire cutter, and screwdriver. You cannot live without such a _____ device.

15. She tends to bend her thoughts back over themselves, thinking constantly. I

have never met such a thoughtful, _____ person.

# Collaborative Work

Answer the following questions.

1. Many companies now have **flextime**. What is this, and for what reasons would a company develop such a plan?

   _____

   _____

2. On the weekend, we often turn our minds to pleasant activities. What such **diversions** do students pursue?

   _____

3. How do the terms **converse** and **conversation** connect to the root's meaning, "to turn"?

   _____

   _____

4. Draw an **inverted** triangle.

5. A common garden flower is the **nasturtium**. Based on a careful analysis of the term, determine how this flower smells.

   _____

   _____

6. How does a **torque** wrench differ from other wrenches?

   _____

   _____

# 21 Roots of Motion V

In this last unit on movement, the roots and words deal with motion that is forced or caused by something. Again, there is an agent (the cause) and an object (something that moves). To push, pull, carry, send, and throw are the important movements here.

## WORD LIST

**port: to carry or move something**

**Example:** Boeing **exports** airplanes. (moves out of the country)

| | | |
|---|---|---|
| deport | export | import |
| port | portable | portage |
| portal | porter | portfolio |
| report | support | transport |

**ject (jac, jet): to throw, place, place near**

**Example:** My body **rejected** the food. (threw it back)

| | | |
|---|---|---|
| adjacent | adjective | dejected |
| eject | inject | interject |
| jet | jettison | project |
| projectile | reject | trajectory |

**pel (puls): to push, force**

**Example:** **Repel** the forces. (push back)

| | | |
|---|---|---|
| compel | compulsive | compulsory |
| dispel | expel | impulse |
| propel | propeller | pulsate |
| pulse | repel | repulsive |

mit (mis): to send, let go, allow

**Example:** **Class is dismissed. (sent away)**

| | | |
|---|---|---|
| admit | commit | dismiss |
| emit | intermission | intermittent |
| messenger | missile | missionary |
| missive | permit | remit |
| submit | | |

tract: to pull, drag

**Example:** **The farmer has a huge tractor. (something that pulls)**

| | | |
|---|---|---|
| attract | contract | detract |
| distract | extract | protract |
| retract | subtract | tractable |
| traction | tractor | |

# Analysis

Many of the words on the Word List are verbs that can be clearly analyzed. Give the verb for the following literal definitions. Then, in the second sentence, put the noun form of the term in the blank. These noun forms are <u>not</u> on the list. The first one has been done for you.

1. "throw back"

   The inflexible union _rejected_ the offer that management made last

   night. After the _rejection_, the workers voted to strike.

2. "carry across"

   The company could not _____ the hazardous waste in that truck.

   The _____ of hazardous waste in that truck is a serious infraction.

3. "send through"

   I cannot _____ you to enter that office.

   You do not have _____ to enter that office.

4. "push out"

The disruptive student was _____ from school.

His _____ tortured his parents.

5. "kick out"

The pitcher was abruptly _____ in the second inning.

After his _____, the Yankees scored six runs.

6. "pull toward"

Opposites _____.

The _____ of opposites happens in physics and love.

7. "push forward"

The Boeing 747 is _____ by four huge engines.

Jet _____ dramatically changed air transportation.

8. "pull out"

The dentist _____ the fragmented tooth.

After the _____, the patient's pain lessened.

9. "carry back"

Get the information and _____ back to me soon.

I hope your _____ is good.

10. "send away"

The class was _____ at the bell.

A huge roar filled the room at _____.

11. "throw between"

My sister always _____ her comments into my conversations with my friends.

Such _____ annoy and interrupt me.

12. "send out"

The sun _____ powerful energies.

Scientists measure these _____ with both simple and complex instruments.

13. "send to (a place)"

This ticket _____ you to the theater.

The price of _____ is $10.

14. "push back"

This will _____ the insects.

Put this _____ on your arms and face.

15. "pull back"

The president _____ his statement.

Even after the _____ of the statement, the controversy raged on.


# Relationships

I.  Complete the following analogies, using words from the Word List.

1.  in : out :: _____ : export

2.  resume : businesswoman :: _____ : artist

3.  _____ : expand :: diminish : grow

4.  add : _____ :: multiply : divide

5.  halftime : football :: _____ : concert

6.  aspirin : swallow :: penicillin : _____

7.  porter : carry :: _____ : pull

8.  wheel : _____ :: automobile : ship

9.  air : jet :: space : _____

10. attractive : _____ :: beautiful : ugly

11. music : beat :: heart : _____

12. _____ : troops :: drop : bomb

13. _____ : noun :: adverb : verb

14. salesperson : product :: _____ : religion

15. impulsive : sudden :: _____ : constant

II. Certain words on the Word List are often used with other terms or phrases.  Rephrase the following into simpler English, changing the boldface terms.

1. **compelled** to tell the truth

_____

2. **dispelled** the rumor

_____

3. **submit** my letter of resignation

_____

4. **remit** payment in thirty days

_____

5. **project** your voice more

_____

6. the **adjacent** building

_____

7. **jettison** the fuel

_____

8. **dejected** in adversity

_____

9. **intermittent** showers are predicted

_____

10. **support** beams of the building

_____

**154**

# Collaborative Work

Answer the following questions and work the following problems.

1.  If an instructor says "Attendance is **compulsory**," how flexible are her policies?

    _____

2.  Where do people go for serious, **protracted** illness? _____

3.  What happens when a car loses **traction**?

    _____

4.  Are most students **tractable**? _____

5.  Could a **messenger** carry a **missive**? _____

6.  What is usually **adjacent** to a large stadium? _____

7.  Why are criminals **deported**?

    _____

8.  When do you **portage** a canoe?

    _____

9.  Name two terms with which you might use **pulsate**.

    a. _____        b. _____

10. Name two ways you might be **distracted** from study.

    a. _____        b. _____

11. Name two ways others might **detract** from your enjoyment of a concert.

    a. _____        b. _____

12. Name two **portable** objects.

    a. _____        b. _____

13. Draw the typical **trajectory** of a **projectile**.

# 22 Roots of Action I

The roots in this unit cover a variety of different human activities or natural actions. While they do not always reflect movement, they are connected to physically doing something.

## WORD LIST

**pos** (**pon**): to put, place, stand

**Example:** I will **compose** a song. (put [notes] together)

| | | |
|---|---|---|
| component | compose | deposit |
| dispose | expose | exposure |
| impose | oppose | position |
| postpone | propose | transpose |

**stru** (**struct**): to build, create; something built or made

**Example:** I will **construct** a bridge. (to build completely)

| | | |
|---|---|---|
| construct | destroy | destruction |
| industry | infrastructure | instruction |
| misconstrue | obstruction | reconstruct |
| structure | superstructure | |

**clos** (**clud**): to close, shut, finish, close off by itself

**Example:** I will **conclude** the essay. (finish completely)

| | | |
|---|---|---|
| claustrophobia | close | closet |
| conclude | disclose | enclose |
| exclude | include | preclude |
| recluse | seclude | |

plic (ply, plex, pli): bend, fold, layer; entwined, knotted; difficult, hard

**Example:**　I will **complicate** matters. (make them very difficult)

| | | |
|---|---|---|
| complex | complicate | explicit |
| implicit | inexplicable | multiply |
| perplex | pleat | pliable |
| pliers | plywood | |

fic (fac, feas, fec): to make, create, produce; something made

**Example:**　This is **counterfeit** money. (opposite of made [true])

| | | |
|---|---|---|
| artifact | counterfeit | defect |
| edifice | effect | facilitate |
| facsimile | factory | feasible |
| fiction | manufacture | perfect |
| profit | | |

# Analysis

Choose a word from the Word List to match the literal definitions.

1. "a place where something is made": _____

   She worked in the missile _____.

2. "something that folds": _____

   I extracted the tooth with a _____.

3. "not able to unfold": _____

   For some _____ reason, she abruptly dismissed class.

4. "able to make": _____

   I won't reject your plan; I think it is _____.

5. "place something together": _____

   Permit me to _____ a song for your anniversary.

6. "end completely": _____

I _____ the report at two in the morning.

7. "place later": _____

The game was _____ because of intermittent heavy rain.

8. "build completely": _____

The tower was _____ in less than a year.

9. "opposite of build": _____

The tower was _____ in less than an hour.

10. "Shut out": _____

The press was _____ from the closed-door meeting.

11. "place out (in something)": _____

We were _____ to repulsive new television shows.

12. "closed off": _____

After the long portage, we found a _____ campsite.

13. "built wrongly": _____

You have _____ what I said about missionaries.

14. "to make completely": _____

We have finally _____ the new propeller.

15. "able to fold": _____

Warm plastic is _____.

# Relationships

I. Complete the following analogies, using words from the Word List.

1. implicit : unstated :: _____ : clearly stated

2. crease : pants :: _____ : skirt

3. divide : lessen :: _____ : increase

4. cause : _____ :: reason : result

5. hospital : physicians :: college : _____

6. car : garage :: clothes : _____

7. _____ : money :: forgery : art

8. bridge : acrophobia :: elevator : _____

9. _____ : favor :: against : for

10. build : construct :: _____ : remodel

II. Below are several complex sentences. Rewrite them in simpler English, choosing synonyms for the boldface words.

1. The **industries** that **manufactured components** for typewriters and adding machines faced a **complicated** dilemma with the advent of computers and electronics. They could either modernize and adapt, or face a loss of **profit** and **position**.

_____

_____

_____

_____

_____

2. I am **perplexed** that the **superstructure** of this **edifice** was **constructed** of **plywood**.

_____

_____

3. The **recluse** lived in a small **structure**, and the path there was filled with **obstructions**.

_____

_____

4. At the **close** of each psychology lecture, the **instructor included** a short piece of **fiction** to illustrate her points.

_____

_____

# Collaborative Work

The following common phrases use terms from the Word List. Explain each phrase in simpler English; then write a sentence including the phrase. In a group, select the strongest, clearest sentence.

1. transport and **dispose** of the garbage

_____

_____

2. die of **exposure**

_____

_____

3. **impose** new taxes

_____

_____

4. **propose** marriage

_____

_____

5. **deposit** the money

_____

_____

6. **transpose** the letters

_____

_____

7. nation's **infrastructure**

_____

_____

8. math **instruction**

_____

_____

9. **enclose** the check

_____

_____

10. **disclose** the truth

_____

_____

11. **facsimile** edition

_____

_____

12. an ancient **artifact**

_____

_____

13. birth **defects**

_____

_____

14. **facilitate** change

_____

_____

# 23 Roots of Action II

The roots in this unit are rarely cheerful; instead, they deal with killing, cutting, ending, dying, and other unpleasant experiences.

## WORD LIST

**cide**: to kill

**Example:**     There was a **homicide** last week. (to kill a human)

| | | |
|---|---|---|
| deciduous | fratricide | genocide |
| germicide | herbicide | homicide |
| infanticide | matricide | patricide |
| pesticide | regicide | suicide |

**mort** (**mor**, **mur**): to die, be killed; death, dying

**Example:**     People are **mortal**. (related to death, able to die)

| | | |
|---|---|---|
| amortize | immortal | immortality |
| immortalize | morbid | morgue |
| moribund | mortal | mortality |
| mortgage | mortician | mortify |
| mortuary | murder | murderous |
| postmortem | | |

**cise** (**sect**, **seg**): to cut; a part cut

**Example:**     Make your speech **concise**. (cut very [short])

| | | |
|---|---|---|
| concise | dissect | excise |
| incision | incisor | intersect |
| precise | scissors | section |
| sector | segment | |

term: end, limit, bound

**Example:** We have reached the **terminal.** (ending place)

| | | |
|---|---|---|
| conterminous | determinate | determine |
| exterminate | interminable | term |
| terminal | terminate | terminology |
| terminus | | |

# Analysis

The root <u>cide</u> almost always means "to kill." Using the Glossary, determine who or what is killed in the following actions.

1. homicide: _____

2. patricide: _____

3. matricide: _____

4. infanticide: _____

5. suicide: _____

6. genocide: _____

7. regicide: _____

8. herbicide: _____

9. pesticide: _____

10. germicide: _____

# Relationships

I.    Complete the following analogies, using words from the Word List.

1. molar : chew :: _____ : cut

2. loan : car :: _____ : house

3. _____ : nursery :: corpse : baby

4. bus : _____ :: ship : port

5. extract : tooth :: _____ : tumor

6. animals : slaughter :: insects : _____

7. concise : short :: _____ : accurate

8. debt : _____ :: savings : grow

9. _____ : animal :: analyze : problem

10. _____ : originate :: end : begin

II. In the sentences, substitute a word from the Word List for the underlined phrase. Then, use that word to write a sentence that has a meaning similar to the original sentence.

1. I have concluded that I will <u>live forever</u>.

   I am _____.

2. His boring lecture on the infrastructure seemed to <u>never end</u>.

   His boring lecture was _____.

3. Eastern Avenue <u>cuts through</u> Lakeside Street near the factory.

   Eastern Avenue _____.

4. You <u>scared me to death</u> with those <u>cutters</u>.

   You _____.

5. The <u>end</u> of the railroad line was in San Diego.

   The railroad's _____.

6. The surgeon made <u>a sharp cut</u> above the heart.

   The surgeon made an _____.

7. In this <u>part</u> of the movie, the hunter gives a <u>deadly</u> blow to the <u>dying</u> deer.

   In this _____

   _____.

8. With a gleam in her eye, she <u>killed her brother</u>.

   She committed _____.

9. Shakespeare's fame <u>will live forever</u> in such lines as "To be or not to be."

   Shakespeare's fame is _____

   _____.

10. Do you think about <u>death</u>?

    Do you _____?

---

**164**

# Collaborative Work

Answer the following questions. First do the exercises alone and then compare your responses to those of your group members.

1.  What is killed in a **deciduous** tree?  When?

    _____

    _____

2.  When, where, why, and by whom are **postmortem** exams done?

    _____

3.  Do you believe in personal **immortality**?  Why?

    _____

4.  What are the 48 **conterminous** states in the United States?

    _____

5.  What is the difference between an **indeterminate** and a **determinate** tomato plant?

    _____

    _____

6.  Do **morticians** work with **moribund** people in the **mortuary**? _____

7.  How are the terms **definition** and **terminology** related to their roots?

    _____

8.  Create a concise sentence for each of the following pairs:

    **section**/book

    _____

    **sector**/city

    _____

    **segment**/show

    _____

# Review IV

Give the meaning of the root; then analyze the boldfaced term and write its literal definition.

**Unit 17**     **Roots of Motion I**

| Root | Meaning | Phrase | Literal Definition |
|------|---------|--------|--------------------|
| cycle | _____ | a **cyclical** problem | _____ |
| mot | _____ | stand **motionless** | _____ |
| ceed | _____ | **exceed** the limit | _____ |
| ven | _____ | **circumvent** the rule | _____ |

**Unit 18**     **Roots of Motion II**

| cur | _____ | a **recurrent** problem | _____ |
| flu | _____ | a clear **fluid** | _____ |
| duc | _____ | **induce** labor | _____ |
| sue | _____ | the **ensuing** problem | _____ |
| grad | _____ | my **gradual** recovery | _____ |

**Unit 19**     **Roots of Motion III**

| tens | _____ | a **tense** moment | _____ |
| strict | _____ | a **strict** budget | _____ |
| joi | _____ | **join** the club | _____ |
| press | _____ | **pressure**-packed game | _____ |

**Unit 20**     **Roots of Motion IV**

| fract | _____ | a bad **fracture** | _____ |

| rupt | _____ | an **abrupt** change | _____ |
| tort | _____ | **distort** the truth | _____ |
| vert | _____ | **revert** to smoking | _____ |
| flect | _____ | **reflect** on problems | _____ |

## Unit 21    Roots of Motion V

| port | _____ | **import** cars | _____ |
| mit | _____ | **emit** energy | _____ |
| ject | _____ | **reject** newcomers | _____ |
| pel | _____ | steam-**propelled** | _____ |
| tract | _____ | **attracted** to light | _____ |

## Unit 22    Roots of Action I

| pos | _____ | **deposit** the money | _____ |
| stru | _____ | **destroy** the virus | _____ |
| clos | _____ | **enclose** a check | _____ |
| plex | _____ | a **complex** problem | _____ |
| fic | _____ | a **fictional** man | _____ |

## Unit 23    Roots of Action II

| cide | _____ | an eerie **homicide** | _____ |
| mort | _____ | our **mortal** life | _____ |
| seg | _____ | the shorter **segment** | _____ |
| term | _____ | **terminal** illness | _____ |

# Review IV: Reading

## A Different Life

Human beings have a strong tendency to move. In the <u>course</u> of history, we have seen great <u>cycles</u> of mass <u>movements</u> of people between countries and continents. As you learned in *Part I* of this text, the ancient <u>ancestors</u> of English-speaking people migrated from southern Europe to northern Europe. The <u>predecessors</u> of the native populations of North and South America came from the Asian continent. For thousands of years, there had been an <u>incessant</u> <u>motion</u> of whole tribes, and this movement <u>gradually</u> <u>permitted</u> human beings to <u>extend</u> themselves throughout the world.

<u>Currently</u>, we see very few of these mass human movements; nevertheless, individuals have not lost their <u>motivation</u> to seek a better life in a different country. There are four basic <u>motives</u> that <u>impel</u> individuals to leave their native land and move thousands of miles to another. One is a clear "pull" to another country, that is, the wish to <u>pursue</u> a more <u>affluent</u> or better life in a new land. The second and third reasons are more a "push" than a "pull": that is, many need to escape political <u>repression</u> and <u>construct</u> a better life elsewhere, while others seek to <u>express</u> and follow a faith free from religious <u>persecution</u> in a more tolerant nation. The last reason, however, is not so much a "push" or a "pull" as it is a "dragging." Some people have been <u>compelled</u> to move to new nations, forced against their will to <u>disrupt</u> their lives forever.

Individuals move to a new country because they are "pulled" or <u>attracted</u> to the chance of a better life. In the nineteenth century, Europeans <u>flooded</u> to Canada and the United States to make farms and work in

<u>factories</u>. In the same century, Chinese moved to North America and Australia seeking financial <u>success</u>. Today, there is an <u>influx</u> of "guest workers" to many nations of Europe. From all over the world, these immigrants have been <u>induced</u> to leave the <u>strain</u> of the <u>extensive</u> poverty of their native land to seek a better life in the <u>productive</u> workplaces in Germany, France, and England. <u>Flexible</u> in their attitudes and <u>versatile</u> in their skills, immigrants who <u>aggressively</u> pursue this better life very often reach their goal.

While the "pull" of a better life in a new country causes many to <u>venture</u> out, others are "pushed" from their native land. In times of civil unrest, freedoms are <u>restricted</u> and laws become <u>stringent</u>. As <u>tension</u> rises, some people, rather than <u>oppose</u> the new government, need to seek safety or refuge in other lands. In times of war or in the <u>subsequent</u> <u>disruptions</u>, the human rights of the defeated people are often <u>destroyed</u>, and they may be <u>expelled</u> from the country. In recent years, we have seen many refugees from such horrible <u>events.</u> Many people fled the <u>distress</u> of Hitler's Germany. Civil wars and revolutions in Iran, Uganda, and Central America created many refugees. When the Soviet Union warred with Afghanistan, and when the United States fought in Vietnam, thousands of refugees were <u>admitted</u> to other nations. Their lives forever <u>complicated</u>, their spirits <u>dejected</u>, and their minds <u>perplexed</u> by all that had happened, the refugees boldly attempted to <u>reconstruct</u> a meaningful life in a foreign land.

The third reason for immigration is again a "push." Basic religious beliefs of people will often come into conflict with <u>inflexible</u> rules of government. In fact, governments will often try to <u>suppress</u> religious freedoms because they threaten the power of the state. <u>Contending</u> with such a choice between church and state, the believer must either <u>submit</u> to the laws of the land or <u>reject</u> the rules and seek religious <u>expression</u> elsewhere. For example, many of the early immigrants to the United States from Europe came because <u>strict</u> laws were <u>imposed</u> on their religious practices. In more recent

times, the Bahais were prevented from following their beliefs and fled Iran; Hindus and Sikhs immigrated from Pakistan to India, while the Muslims escaped religious pressures in India and moved to Pakistan. The deep human impulse to conduct one's life according to religious convictions has promoted much emigration.

While wars and religious persecution cause great upheaval and force people to move, the most torturous reason for human movement is to be "dragged" from one's native land into slavery in another. As in the case of the English deporting criminals to Australia and Europeans capturing and transporting Africans to America, people are moved against their will. The slave trade was an especially repulsive moment in human history. Exposed to adverse conditions both on the slave fleets and in America, these men, women, and children were oppressed as few groups of people ever have been. In fact, the whole idea of slavery was such a perversion of human rights that the controversy it generated intensified into the Civil War. Yet even today, African Americans struggle to gain a position in American society that other groups have long enjoyed.

Once the immigrants arrive in a new land, their life does not abruptly change for the better. Sometimes, if their new country has a shortage of workers, the newcomers are welcomed and their entry is facilitated by generous laws. In such cases, little prevents the immigrant from making economic progress. On the other hand, if the numbers of workers exceeds the number of jobs, the immigrants feel great rejection from the people already living there. In fact, racist mobs have murdered immigrants out of fear they would take their jobs away. In addition, living in a new land, becoming fluent in a new language, and adapting to a new culture while maintaining the traditions of the former culture amount to an enormously stressful way to live.

Yet despite the initial and subsequent problems most immigrants face, the desire to move and improve one's life has not been reduced in recent years. And perhaps you in your lifetime, or your children in theirs, will see the busy ports or crowded concourses of new land and unrestricted opportunity.

## Questions

1. Return to the text and circle any underlined terms that you don't know. Try to analyze and form a literal definition for these terms by using the Glossary. If you still cannot form a clear definition, have a member of your group help you.

2. Write a short paragraph in which you compare the reasons you immigrated (or might decide to immigrate) to another country with the reasons given in the reading.

3. Look back to the word lists in Units 17–23. Using at least twenty words from the lists, write a short essay on one of the following topics:

    a. Stress in Your Life

    b. Sports and the Injuries They Cause

    c. Travel

    d. Death

# V

# Roots of
# Human
# Activity

# 24 Roots of the Senses I

Human beings are usually said to have five senses: sight, smell, touch, hearing, and taste. The roots in this unit involve words related to speech and hearing.

## WORD LIST

<u>voc</u> (<u>vok</u>): to call, speak

**Example:** We argued **vociferously.** (full of [loud] speaking)

| | | |
|---|---|---|
| advocate | convocation | equivocate |
| evoke | invoke | irrevocable |
| provoke | revoke | vocal |
| vocation | vociferous | voice |

<u>dic</u> (<u>dict</u>): to speak, say, tell, command

**Example:** Don't **contradict** me. (speak the opposite)

| | | |
|---|---|---|
| abdicate | benediction | contradict |
| dictate | dictator | diction |
| dictionary | dictum | ditty |
| edict | malediction | predict |
| valedictorian | verdict | |

<u>clam</u> (<u>claim</u>): to talk, shout, demand

**Example:** There arose a **clamor.** (a shout)

| | | |
|---|---|---|
| claim | claimant | clamor |
| clamorous | declaim | disclaim |
| exclaim | proclaim | reclaim |

log (loc, loqu): to speak, talk

**Example:**     **We had an interesting dialogue.** (two people talking)

| | | |
|---|---|---|
| circumlocution | colloquial | colloquium |
| dialogue | elocution | eloquent |
| grandiloquent | interlocutor | loquacious |
| magniloquent | monologue | soliloquy |
| somniloquent | ventriloquist | |

chor: to sing; to dance

**Example:**     **Choral** music is beautiful. (related to singing)

| | | |
|---|---|---|
| carol | choir | choral |
| chorale | chord | choreographer |
| chorus | | |

# Analysis

Analyze each boldface term and write a literal definition.

1. "I won! I won!" **exclaimed** the holder of the lucky lottery ticket.

   _____

2. "Please don't **contradict** me," sighed the perplexed parent.

   _____

3. The tribe encircled the tree and **invoked** the blessing of the gods.

   _____

4. The judge **revoked** my driver's license and imposed a heavy fine after my third infraction.

   _____

5. At the conclusion of the trial, the jury's **verdict** was "not guilty."

   _____

6. The mayor **declaimed** in a **grandiloquent** manner on the beauty of the edifice.

   _____

7. His angry, explicit words **provoked** many to fight.

   _____

8. After a bottle of wine, she became quite **loquacious**.

   _____

9. The smells of kimchi **evoked** memories of Seoul.

   _____

10. The mortician was happy in his **vocation**.

    _____

11. I **disclaim** any knowledge of the homicide.

    _____

12. I was mortified by my words, but they were **irrevocable**.

    _____

13. Her **diction** was precise.

    _____

14. I couldn't study in the interminable **clamor** of the cafeteria.

    _____

15. Einstein was **proclaimed** the greatest mind of the twentieth century.

    _____

# Relationships

I. There are many types of people and professions on the Word List. Choose words to fit the descriptions below.

   1. She is the one who speaks for you in court. This lawyer is your _____.

   2. He is the one who speaks words of worth and value at graduation. He is the class

      _____.

3. She is the one who demands what is rightfully hers. In this court case, she is the

_____ .

4. He is the ruler of a country, and whatever he says, everyone does. Hitler, Nero, and

Idi Amin were all _____.

5. She writes the instructions for the dancers. Twyla Tharp is a well-known

_____.

6. He seems to speak from his stomach, and he carries a puppet or dummy. He is a

_____ .

7. She is the go-between for lovers, sharing in conversations and delivering messages. She is the _____.

II. Complete the following analogies.

1. remember : past :: _____ : future

2. blessing : benediction :: curse : _____

3. boss : _____ :: assistant : write

4. _____ : one :: dialogue : two

5. guitar : instrumental :: voice : _____

6. eloquent : audience :: _____ : friends

7. vociferous : _____ :: noisy : loud

8. library : books :: _____ : words

9. throne : _____ :: presidency : resign

10. lead : regain :: title : _____

III. Write a sentence for each phrase.

1. Christmas **carol**

_____

**2.** church **choir**

_____

**3.** **choral** music

_____

**4.** symphony **chorale**

_____

**5.** major **chord**

_____

**6.** the **chorus** line

_____

# Collaborative Work

In a group or with a partner, explain the difference between or among the boldface terms, and then answer the questions.

**1. edict, dictum, ditty**

    **a.** Match the phrases to the words.

        _____ **1.** Honor thy father and mother.

        _____ **2.** All streets must be clear by 11 P.M. Violators will be arrested.

        _____ **3.** Hey diddle diddle; the cat and the fiddle; the cow jumped over the moon.

**2. circumlocution, equivocation, elocution**

    **a.** Who might do each? Why? When?

_____

_____

_____

3. **convocation, colloquium**

   a.  When might each occur? Why?

   _____

   _____

   _____

4. **magniloquent** speaker, **somniloquent** speaker

   a.  Who might do each? Why?

   _____

   _____

   _____

**177**

# 25 Roots of the Senses II

In this unit, you will learn the roots connected to sight, sound, and touch. (There are only a few roots connected to smell or taste, and they include  nas: nose, nasal, nostril; odor: odor, malodorous, odorless; and flav: flavor, unflavorable.)

## WORD LIST

spect (spis): to see, watch, observe, look

**Example:** I **speculate** that I will win. (look into [the future])

| | | |
|---|---|---|
| circumspect | despise | expect |
| inspect | perspective | prospect |
| retrospect | speck | spectacles |
| spectator | specter | speculate |
| suspect | | |

vid (vis): to see, watch, observe, look

**Example:** My **supervisor** is great. (one who watches over)

| | | |
|---|---|---|
| envision | evident | invisible |
| provide | review | revise |
| supervisor | television | video |
| videotape | vision | visitor |
| visual | | |

aud: to hear, listen, sound

**Example:** The **audio** portion is gone. (sound)

| | | |
|---|---|---|
| audience | audio | audiobook |
| audiolingual | audiophile | audiovisual |
| audition | auditor | auditorium |
| auditory | inaudible | |

phon: sound, hearing

**Example:** The birds are **cacophonous.** (full of bad sounds)

| | | |
|---|---|---|
| cacophony | euphony | headphone |
| megaphone | microphone | phonetics |
| symphony | telephone | |

tach (tact, tang): to touch, connect, feel by touch

**Example:** The disease is **contagious.** ([spread by] touching together)

| | | |
|---|---|---|
| attach | contact | contagious |
| contiguous | detach | intangible |
| tact | tactile | tangent |
| tangible | tangled | |

# Analysis

Choose a word from the Word List to match the following literal definition.

1. "not able to touch"            _____ assets

2. "not able to be heard"         _____ voices

3. "not able to be seen"          _____ ink

4. "one who hears"                _____ in this class

5. "one who (comes to) see"       _____ to this city

6. "one who oversees"             _____ at work

7. "one who watches"              _____ at the track meet

8. "one who is watched from below" _____ of the police

9. "one who loves to hear (music)" _____ of choral music

10. "look into"                   _____ the luggage

11. "look for"                    _____ for gold

12. "to make a sight (in the mind)" _____ the future

13. "touching together"           _____ disease

14. "touch together"        _____ my lawyer

15. "touching together"      _____ forty-eight states

# Relationships

I.   Complete the following analogies, using words from the Word List.

1. stadium : auditorium :: spectators : _____

2. connect : attach :: _____ : separate

3. rock band : _____ :: job : interview

4. _____ : watch :: CD : listen

5. sight : _____ :: hearing : auditory

6. eye : _____ :: ear : audio

7. finger : ear :: _____ : auditory

8. peep : ear :: _____ : eye

9. sight : sound :: television : _____

10. grammar : writing :: _____ : speech

II.   In each set of sentences, choose a word from the Word List for the blank to make the two sentences have related meanings. The literal definition for the unknown word is in the first sentence.

1. The choreographer had a nice touch with the dancers.

   Such _____ made her quite popular.

2. All the sounds blended together warmly.

   The _____ was beautiful.

3. The dictator could clearly see that all were fearful.

   Fear was _____ on each person's face.

4. Looking back, I could see my mistake.

   In _____, I could see the error was irrevocable.

5. The dramatist needed to look at the scene again.

   She needs to _____ it before tomorrow's premiere.

6. I need to look at this chapter again.

   I hope the _____ will help me pass the exam.

7. I look down on what you have said.

   And I _____ what you have done.

8. My hair is all twisted and touching.

   I have a _____ mess.

9. Look around before you make a big prediction.

   You need to be _____ when you claim to know the future.

10. I hope to get a more complete view of the issue at the colloquium.

    Such a broader _____ helps me solve my problems.


# Collaborative Work

First alone and then in a group, do the following problems or answer the following questions.

1. Explain what the following items are or do:

   a.  audiobook

   _____

   b.  videotape

   _____

   c.  audiolingual tapes

   _____

   d.  audiovisual equipment

   _____

**e.** megaphone

_____

**f.** microphone

_____

**g.** headphone

_____

**h.** spectacles

_____

2. Write a sentence for each of the following words, using the word <u>future</u> in each sentence.

    **a.** expect

    _____

    **b.** speculate

    _____

    **c.** provide

    _____

    **d.** vision

    _____

    **e.** specter

    _____

3. Explain the difference between **cacophony** and **euphony**. In what situations would you hear each?

_____

_____

_____

4. Draw a circle.  Draw a line **tangent** to the circle. Based on your drawing, explain what it means "to go off on a tangent?"

_____

_____

5. What are the **tangible** assets of a corporation?

_____

# 26 Roots of Life Processes I

In this unit, most of the roots are related to the processes of birth and life. In addition, words that classify living organisms are also introduced.

## WORD LIST

**bio:** life

**Example:** I will take **Biology** 101 next year. (the study of life)

| | | |
|---|---|---|
| aerobic | amphibious | antibiotic |
| autobiography | biodegradable | biofeedback |
| biography | biology | biopsy |
| biosphere | microbial | symbiotic |

**viv (vit):** life

**Example:** These kids are so **vivacious.** (full of life)

| | | |
|---|---|---|
| convivial | revive | survive |
| viable | vital | vitality |
| vitamin | vivacious | vivid |
| vivisection | | |

**nat:** life, birth, groups of living beings

**Example:** Breathing is **innate.** (in at birth)

| | | |
|---|---|---|
| impregnate | innate | naive |
| natal | nation | native |
| nativity | nature | naturopathy |
| neonatal | pregnant | prenatal |
| renaissance | | supernatural |

# Analysis

Choose a word from the Word List that matches the literal definition and fits logically into the phrases.

1. _____ "live through"    _____ the accident;

   _____ the exam

2. _____ "above nature"    _____ world of ghosts and specters;

   _____ powers

3. _____ "bring back to life" _____ the swimmer;

   _____ the lost art

4. _____ "(present) in birth"_____ ability to breathe;

   _____ a desire to live

5. _____ "to make grow"    _____ the seed

6. _____ "to kill a race"    Hitler's policy of _____;

   _____ of Native Americans

7. _____ "of the same type"    _____ milk;

   _____ beliefs

8. _____ "to grow back"    _____ a tail;

   _____ a limb

9. _____ "completely alive"    _____ neighbors;

   _____ personality

10. _____ "small life"    _____ life;

    _____ organism

11. _____ "able to live"    _____ fetus;

    _____ seeds

12. _____ "a birth again"    _____ art;

    the Italian _____

13. _____ "a common type"    _____ foods;

    _____ cigarettes;

    _____ food labels

14. _____ "opposite of grow"    _____ into chaos;

    begin to _____

15. _____ "to make grow"    _____ good will;

    _____ hate

# Relationships

I.    Complete the following analogies, using words from the Word List.

1.  happy : _____ :: morose : sad

2. interbreeding : animals :: _____ : humans

3. child : _____ :: elder : wise

4. ending : termination :: beginning : _____

5. _____ : electricity :: compose : music

6. pedigree : animal :: _____ : humans

7. state : part :: _____ : whole

8. others : biography :: self : _____

9. _____ : specific :: broad : narrow

10. impregnate : prenatal :: nativity : _____

11. _____ : foreign :: born : immigrant

12. nurture : _____ :: learned : innate

13. vivacious : lively :: _____ : lifelike

II. Many of the terms on the Word List are commonly used in the biological and medical sciences. Match the boldface words or phrases in **A** to their explanations in **B**.

**Biological Sciences**

| A | B |
|---|---|
| _____ 1. the **biosphere** | A. a type or group of animals |
| _____ 2. **symbiotic** relationship | B. changing heredity to improve a life form |
| _____ 3. **biodegradable** substance | C. changing heredity to improve a life form |
| _____ 4. **genetic** engineering | D. requiring air to live |
| _____ 5. **eugenic** experiments | E. living on both land and water |
| _____ 6. **indigenous** species | F. the study of all life |
| _____ 7. **Genus**: Canis | G. the entire living world |
| _____ 8. plant **biology** | H. born in or native to an area |
| _____ 9. **aerobic** organism | I. able to break down naturally |
| _____ 10. **amphibious** creature | J. two life forms helping each other |

187

**Medical Sciences**

| | | | |
|---|---|---|---|
| _____ | 1. **antibiotic** | A. | cutting open a live animal |
| _____ | 2. **biofeedback** | B. | examining living tissue |
| _____ | 3. **biopsy** | C. | reproductive body parts |
| _____ | 4. **vitamin** pill | D. | heart rate, breath, blood pressure |
| _____ | 5. **vivisection** | E. | present at birth |
| _____ | 6. **genital** organs | F. | cancer-causing material |
| _____ | 7. **pathogenic** organism | G. | disease-causing microbes |
| _____ | 8. **vital signs** | H. | a destroyer of microorganisms |
| _____ | 9. **congenital** disease | I. | treating disease holistically |
| _____ | 10. **naturopathy** | J. | listening to and altering body processes |
| _____ | 11. **carcinogenic** substance | K. | essential organic chemical |

# Collaborative Work

The root **gen** is complex, for it has a variety of meanings. However, the meanings are related. Sometimes the root has to do with birth or physical characteristics of the family, but families often form tribes, so the root extended itself to mean groups of related people or races, and since members of a tribe or race develop a culture, the root stretched further to describe how members of the same tribe treated each other. Below is a list of words, each with the **gen** root. Place them into the correct category.

| | | | | | |
|---|---|---|---|---|---|
| **gene** | **gentle** | **progeny** | **generous** | **generation** | **genocide** |
| **gentry** | **gender** | **genital** | **genotype** | **progenitor** | **heterogenous** |
| **genial** | **genteel** | **genetics** | **congenital** | **genealogy** | **miscegenation** |

1. Words related to birth, heredity, and physical characteristics:

   _____

   _____

   _____

   _____

2. Words related to tribes, races, or related families:

_____

_____

_____

_____

3. Words related to treatment of members of the same group:

_____

_____

_____

_____

# 27 Roots of Life Processes II

Some of the roots in this unit are connected to our physical life, while others are connected to our mental and emotional life.

## WORD LIST

---

card: heart, mind, feeling

**Example:** I **encourage** you to study. (to make a [strong] feeling)

| | | |
|---|---|---|
| accord | cardiac | cardialgia |
| cardiology | cordial | core |
| courageous | discord | discourage |
| electrocardiogram | encourage | |

---

corp: body, organization

**Example:** I am against **corporal** punishment. (related to the body)

| | | |
|---|---|---|
| corporal | corporation | corps |
| corpse | corpulent | corpuscle |
| incorporeal | | |

---

path: feeling, emotion; disease, sickness

**Example:** I am **apathetic** about the election. (lacking any feeling)

| | | |
|---|---|---|
| antipathy | apathetic | apathy |
| compassion | compatible | empathy |
| passion | passionate | passive |
| pathetic | pathogen | pathology |
| patient | psychopath | sympathetic |
| sympathy | | |

---

**sent**: feeling, perception, thought

**Example:** The **sentry** was awakened. (one who perceives)

| | | |
|---|---|---|
| assent | sentinel | sentry |
| insensitive | consent | dissent |
| sense | presentiment | resent |
| sensual | senseless | sensorimotor |
| sensuous | sentient | sentiments |

# Analysis

Analyze and write a literal definition of the following boldface terms. Then use the word or phrase in a sentence.

1. **electrocardiogram**

   _____

   _____

2. **cordial** welcome

   _____

   _____

3. **cardiac** failure

   _____

   _____

4. **corporal** punishment

   _____

   _____

5. rotting **corpse**

   _____

   _____

6. **incorporeal** spirit

_____

_____

7. **apathetic** students

_____

_____

8. **compatible** roommates

_____

_____

9. **psychopathic** killer

_____

_____

10. **passionate** speech

_____

_____

11. **sympathetic** listener

_____

_____

12. **dissenting** votes

_____

_____

13. **presentiment** of death

_____

_____

14. **sentient** animal

_____

_____

15. **sensorimotor** skills

_____

_____

# Relationships

I.   Complete the following analogies, using words from the Word List.

1.  war : peace :: _____ : concord

2.  skinny : slim :: _____ : obese

3.  rind : outside :: _____ : inside

4.  military : _____ :: city : police

5.  cardiology : heart :: _____ : disease

6.  _____ : Marine :: flock : bird

7.  passive : _____ :: weak : strong

8.  love : fondness :: distaste : _____

9.  assent : _____ :: agree : accord

10. encourage : achievement :: _____ : failure

II.  A root's literal meaning will often be stretched to include related meanings. <u>Path</u> means "disease" (a sick feeling), but it has come to mean any feeling. Choose the four <u>card</u> words that refer to your physical heart, the four <u>corp</u> words that refer to the human body, and the three <u>path</u> words that refer to disease.

| | | |
|---|---|---|
| 1. _____ | 1. _____ | 1. _____ |
| 2. _____ | 2. _____ | 2. _____ |
| 3. _____ | 3. _____ | 3. _____ |
| 4. _____ | 4. _____ | |

# Collaborative Work

Answer the following questions or work the following problems. Do them alone and then discuss them in a group.

1.  Would a **cardiologist** be interested in **corpuscles**? Why?

    _____

    _____

2.  In what **sense** is a **corporation** a body or person?

    _____

    _____

3.  Are great actors and actresses filled with **apathy** or **passion**? _____

4.  Explain the differences among **empathy**, **sympathy**, and **compassion**.

    _____

    _____

    _____

5.  Explain the difference between a **sensual** and **sensuous** experience.

    _____

    _____

6.  Rewrite the following without using a word with a <u>sent</u> root. "I **resent** your **sentiments**, and I **sense** you are **insensitive** to such **senseless** crimes."

    _____

    _____

    _____

7.  Rewrite the following without using a word with a <u>card</u> root. "The prime minister **encouraged** the leaders to reach an **accord**."

    _____

    _____

    _____

8. Rewrite the following without using a word with a <u>path</u> root. "We had **compassion** for the **pathetic**, abandoned child."

_____

_____

_____

# 28 Roots of Mental Activity

Our ability to think about and remember words, ideas, and events is an important part of our life. In this unit, the key mental jobs of thinking, remembering, believing, questioning, knowing, teaching, and learning are explored.

## WORD LIST

**ment (mon):** to think; mind, thought

**Example:** That man is **demented.** (away from [normal] mind)

| | | |
|---|---|---|
| demented | mental | mentality |
| mentor | mind | mindless |
| monument | premonition | remind |
| reminder | | |

**cred:** to believe, trust

**Example:** I give little **credence** to your excuse. (state of belief)

| | | |
|---|---|---|
| credence | credentials | credible |
| credit | credo | credulous |
| creed | discredit | incredible |

**mem (mnes):** to remember, recall; memory

**Example:** I have a poor **memory** for names. (a place for recalling)

| | | |
|---|---|---|
| amnesia | amnesty | commemoration |
| immemorial | memento | memo |
| memoirs | memorabilia | memorable |
| memorial | memory | mnemonic |
| remember | reminisce | |

**gnos**: to know, think, be aware, attend to

**Example:**     I am **cognizant** of your pain. (aware of)

| | | |
|---|---|---|
| agnostic | cognition | cognizant |
| connoisseur | diagnose | ignorance |
| ignore | prognosis | prognosticate |
| recognize | reconnaissance | |

**qui** (**que**, **quar**): to ask, seek, strive, fight, win

**Example:**     I have a **question**. (state of asking something)

| | | |
|---|---|---|
| conquer | conquest | conquistador |
| inquest | inquire | inquisition |
| inquisitive | quarrel | querulous |
| query | quest | question |
| questionnaire | quiz | request |

**doc** (**dog**, **doc**): teach, belief, knowledge, opinion

**Example:**     Learn this **doctrine**. (what is believed)

| | | |
|---|---|---|
| disciple | docent | docile |
| doctor | doctrine | docudrama |
| dogma | dogmatic | heterodox |
| indoctrinate | orthodox | paradox |

**leg** (**lec**, **lex**): to gather, choose, read

**Example:**     **Dyslexia** is a reading problem. (poor reading)

| | | |
|---|---|---|
| collect | dialect | dyslexia |
| eclectic | elect | illegible |
| intellect | lectern | lecture |
| neglect | predilection | select |

# Analysis

Below are the literal definitions of words from the Word List. Choose the best word to match the definition and to fit logically in the sentences.

1.  "not able to believe": _____

    She told passionate yet _____ stories.

Though corpulent, he has _____ strength.

2. "state of not knowing": _____

    _____ of pathology can increase the spread of contagious diseases.

    _____ and prejudice may create antipathy between people.

3. "gather together": _____

    I _____ coins. The state _____ taxes.

4. "related to the mind": _____

    I made _____ mistakes. I work with _____ health

    patients.

5. "state of believing": _____

    I give no _____ to your presentiments. The instructor gave little

    _____ to the student's incredible story.

6. "able to recall": _____

    My 21st birthday was a _____ event. Thank you for a

    _____ weekend.

7. "to know again": _____

    I _____ your face but forget your name.

    We _____ the sentry.

8. "knowing the future": _____

    The _____ was discouraging. The cardiologist, however, gave a

    hopeful _____ to the patient.

9. "to not know or be aware": _____

    _____ what insensitive liars tell you. He _____ the

    red light and hit another car.

10. "correct teaching": _____

He was an _____ Jew. His beliefs on corporal punishment are not

_____ in the educational community.

11. "prior thought of the future": _____

I had a _____ of a bad accident. My dreams are filled with

_____.

12. "without thought": _____

I made a _____ mistake. When I make _____ er-

rors, I don't look for sympathy.

13. "tending to ask": _____

Children are _____ about the world. She gave me an

_____ yet empathetic look.

14. "not able to read": _____

Your penmanship is _____. The note is scrawled and

_____.

15. "state of lacking memory": _____

I had _____ after my accident. I have temporary

_____ during exams.

# Relationships

In each group of words, circle the one that does not belong, and then determine the category into which the others logically fit.

1. inquire    request    quarrel    query    question

   Category: _____

2. quiz    inquisition    questionnaire    inquest    conquest

   Category: _____

3. reminder   memo   memento   amnesty   memorabilia

   Category: _____

4. monument   memorial   commemoration   credentials

   Category: _____

5. dialect   mind   mentality   memory   intellect   cognition

   Category: _____

6. mentor   disciple   connoisseur   docent   doctor

   Category: _____

7. doctrine   dogma   creed   credo   predilection

   Category: _____

8. remember   prognosticate   reminisce   remind

   Category: _____

9. neglect   select   elect

   Category: _____

# Collaborative Work

I.   Evaluate whether the following statements are true or false and compare and discuss your responses in a group.

_____   1.   Lawyers seek **credible** witnesses for trials.

_____   2.   Psychopaths are **demented**.

_____   3.   Biographers write **memoirs** of famous people.

_____   4.   Lawyers will **discredit** a witness not **cognizant** of the facts.

_____   5.   Salespeople dislike **credulous** buyers.

_____   6.   Dictators encourage **heterodox** beliefs in their countries.

_____   7.   Bombs are often dropped by planes on a **reconnaissance** mission.

_____   8.   **Docile** children are often **querulous**.

_____ 9. **Lectures** are often delivered at a **lectern**.

_____ 10. **Docudramas** entertain and teach.

_____ 11. **Dyslexics** read well.

_____ 12. "The first shall be last" is a **paradox**.

_____ 13. **Eclectic** readers read a variety of books.

_____ 14. **Dogmatic** people attempt to **indoctrinate**.

_____ 15. **Credit** is given to you if the bank believes you can repay.

II. Answer the following questions or do the following problems.

1. The **conquistadors**, in **quest** of gold, **conquered** what countries?

_____

_____

2. What is the difference between an **agnostic** and an atheist?

_____

_____

3. Explain the difference between a **diagnosis** and a **prognosis**.

_____

_____

4. What is a **mnemonic** device?  Give an example.

_____

_____

5. What has existed since time **immemorial**?

_____

_____

# 29 Roots of Qualities

Virtually all objects and beings have qualities or characteristics that make them different from other objects or beings. Strong, clear, hard, full, worth, and pleasing are a few of the characteristics introduced in this unit.

## WORD LIST

**fort**: strong, safe

**Example:**    I admire her **fortitude.** (state of being strong)

| | | |
|---|---|---|
| comfort | discomfort | effort |
| enforce | force | fort |
| forte | fortification | fortify |
| fortissimo | fortitude | fortress |
| reinforce | | |

**clar**: clear, bright, beautiful

**Example:**    I admire his **clarity** of mind. (state of being clear)

| | | |
|---|---|---|
| clairvoyance | claret | clarified |
| clarify | clarinet | clarion |
| clarity | clear | declaration |
| eclair | | |

**dur**: hard, strong, lasting, continuing

**Example:**    The battery is **durable.** (able to last a long time)

| | | |
|---|---|---|
| durability | durable | duration |
| duress | during | endure |
| obdurate | | |

**grat**: pleasing, thankful, free, freely given

**Example:**    This will **gratify** your taste. (to please)

| | | |
|---|---|---|
| congratulate | grace | graceful |
| gracious | grateful | gratify |
| gratis | gratitude | gratuity |
| ingrate | | |

**sat**: full, having enough, complete

**Example:**    My appetite is **insatiable**. (not able to get enough)

| | | |
|---|---|---|
| insatiable | sate | satiate |
| satisfy | saturate | saturation |

**val**:  worthy, strong

**Example:**    Could you **evaluate** this essay? (to determine the worth)

| | | |
|---|---|---|
| ambivalent | avail | convalescent |
| devalue | equivalent | evaluate |
| invalid | invaluable | valetudinarian |
| valiant | validate | valorous |
| valuable | | |

# Analysis

Analyze and give a literal definition for the following terms. Then use each word in a sentence along with the suggested word.

1.  fortify: _____

    vitamin _____

2.  clarify: _____

    memory _____

3.  gratify: _____

    mentor _____

4.  satisfy: _____

    requirements _____

5.  evaluate: _____

    questionnaire _____

6.  discomfort: _____

    incredible _____

7.  durability: _____

    carpet _____

8.  grateful: _____

    doctor _____

9.  graceful: _____

    dancer _____

10. gracious: _____

    request _____

11. insatiable: _____

    desire _____

12. equivalent: _____

    amount _____

13. valuable: _____

    memento _____

14. devalue: _____

    currency _____

15. invalid: _____

    argument _____

# Relationships

I.  Many of the words on the Word List are commonly used with other words. Analyze
    the boldface terms and use each phrase in a sentence.

1. **enforce** the rules _____

_____

2. **reinforce** the troops _____

_____

3. intestinal **fortitude** _____

_____

4. **clarity** of writing _____

_____

5. **clarified** butter _____

_____

6. under **duress** _____

_____

7. **obdurate** pride _____

_____

8. given "**gratis**" _____

_____

9. **grace** period _____

_____

10. **saturation** bombing _____

_____

11. **sate** the senses _____

_____

12. **convalescent** home _____

_____

13. **ambivalent** feelings _____

_____

14. **validate** my feelings _____

_____

15. to no **avail** _____

_____

16. for the **duration** _____

_____

17. **force** feed _____

_____

18. minimal **effort** _____

_____

19. **invaluable** photograph _____

_____

II. Complete the following analogies, using words from the Word List.

1. loud : _____ :: soft : pianissimo

2. feel : premonition :: see : _____

3. courageous : brave :: valorous : _____

4. comfort : loser :: _____ : winner

5. fill : tank :: _____ : sponge

6. treaty : peace :: _____ : war

7. kind : rude :: friend : _____

8. _____ : pain :: enjoy : pleasure

9. pre- : ante- :: _____ : while

10. weak : strong :: worn out : _____

# Collaborative Work

Answer the following questions.

1. Are all **invalids valetudinarians**?

   _____

2. When might you feel **satiated**?

   _____

3. In what ways does a **gratuity** reflect **gratitude**?

   _____

4. In what ways are **eclairs**, **clarets**, **clarions**, and **clarinets** connected to <u>clear</u>?

   _____

   _____

   _____

   _____

5. What are the differences among **fort**, **fortress**, and **fortification**?

   _____

   _____

   _____

6. What is your academic **forte**?

   _____

# 30 Abstract Roots

A few roots in English begin as very simple ideas but become complex over time. For example, you know that <u>ply</u> means "to fold or layer." But over time, this came to mean "folded and layered and all mixed together"; and soon, because items mixed together become tangled and messy, the root came to mean "difficult or complex." This often happens in language: simple roots become more complex over time. In the definitions of the roots below, notice how the meanings move from the simple to the more complex.

## WORD LIST

---

<u>pend</u>: hang, be heavy, be connected, "hanging in time," need, important, "weighty"

**Example:** Children **depend** on their parents. (need)

| | | |
|---|---|---|
| appendix | depend | dependent |
| impending | interdependent | pendant |
| pending | pensive | ponder |
| suspend | | |

---

<u>stat</u> (<u>stit</u>, <u>sist</u>): stand, remain, last, be in a certain condition; something that stands or remains

**Example:** He **persists** in smoking. (keep [smoking] over time)

| | | |
|---|---|---|
| circumstance | consistently | constant |
| constitute | desist | insist |
| institute | obstacle | persist |
| resistance | statue | substitute |
| superstition | | |

---

<u>cap</u> (<u>cep</u>, <u>cip</u>, <u>ceive</u>): take, hold, contain, take or hold in the mind

**Example:** I **accept** your gift. (take to me)

| | | |
|---|---|---|
| accept | anticipate | capacity |
| capsule | captivate | captive |
| captor | capture | conceive |
| intercept | perception | receive |
| recipient | | |

---

# Analysis

Give a literal definition for the following terms so that your definition fits the meaning of the word in the sentence.

1.  signify: _____

    This diploma **signifies** that you have earned a degree.

2.  abstain: _____

    **Abstain** from alcohol if you plan to keep clarity of mind.

3.  capacity: _____

    The fuel tank's **capacity** is fifty liters.

4.  resistance: _____

    Martin Luther King, Jr. fortified his words with nonviolent **resistance**.

5.  pending: _____

    The final decision is **pending** while the officials validate the votes.

6. assignment: _____

   Your **assignment** is to evaluate this essay.

7. detain: _____

   We were **detained** at customs for three hours.

8. accept: _____

   I **accept** the award with gratitude.

9. obstacle: _____

   What are the **obstacles** to your convalescence?

10. suspend: _____

    The durable rope was **suspended** from the ceiling.

11. design: _____

    The children drew complex **designs**.

12. retain: _____

    Although my desire to read is insatiable, I cannot **retain** all that I read.

13. captivate: _____

    The clarity of the poet's voice **captivated** the crowd.

14. institute: _____

    Newly independent nations **institute** new governments.

15. appendix: _____

    The text contained three **appendices**.

# Relationships

I.  Explain the difference in meaning in each group of sentences.

   1. She **attained** her goal of running two miles a day.

      _____

She **maintained** her goal of running two miles a day.

_____

She **pondered** her goal of running two miles a day.

_____

2. He **persisted** in breaking the speed limit.

_____

He **desisted** from breaking the speed limit.

_____

He **insisted** on breaking the speed limit.

_____

3. I **substituted** the plan from the Energy Department.

_____

I **received** the plan from the Energy Department.

_____

I **conceived** the plan from the Energy Department.

_____

I **obtained** the plan from the Energy Department.

_____

II.   Complete the following analogies, using words from the Word List.

   1.  rent : mortgage :: _____ : owner

   2.  donor : donates :: _____ : receives

   3.  pin : _____ :: attach : hang

   4.  painter : sculptor :: portrait : _____

   5.  sign : constant :: _____ : changeable

   6.  police : criminal :: captor : _____

7. _____ : letter :: signet : document

8. interrupt : _____ :: conversation : message

9. _____ : actual :: anticipate : experience

10. _____ : tenet :: irrational : rational

# Collaborative Work

Rewrite each of the following sentences into simpler English, changing the boldface terms. Do them alone first and then compare your responses in groups.

1. The **tenured** professor **tenaciously** tried to **sustain untenable** ideas.

   _____

   _____

2. The **circumstances** are **dependent** upon our **perceptions**.

   _____

   _____

3. The **contents** of the **capsule** were **captured** on film.

   _____

   _____

4. The **pensive** student **consistently continued** to **attend** class.

   _____

   _____

5. The growing **interdependence** of nations **constitutes** the challenge of the next century.

   _____

   _____

6. I **anticipate constant** rain for the next week.

_____

_____


7. The **captor** found the stolen **signet** ring in his enemy's bag.

_____

_____

# Roots of Law and Society I

Because people live in groups and societies, and because this often creates problems and opportunities, many words in the language refer to that part of our life. This unit introduces words about the formal rules that govern our individual and collective actions.

## WORD LIST

**jus** (**jud**, **jur**): correct, fair; evaluate; court

**Example:** Who will **adjudicate** this case? (evaluate in court)

| | | |
|---|---|---|
| adjudicate | adjustment | injustice |
| judge | judgement | judicial |
| judicious | jurisdiction | jurist |
| juror | jury | justice |
| misjudge | perjury | prejudice |

**leg**: law

**Example:** Write to your **legislator.** (one who makes laws)

| | | |
|---|---|---|
| illegal | illegitimate | law |
| lawyer | legal | legalese |
| legalize | legislate | legislation |
| legislator | legislature | legitimate |

**crim**: wrongdoing, something wrong or bad

**Example:** Speeding is a **crime.** (wrongdoing)

| | | |
|---|---|---|
| crime | criminal | criminogenic |
| criminology | decriminalize | discriminate |
| incriminate | | |

**pen**: to hurt, harm; to be sorry for an action

**Example:**   The criminal was **impenitent.** (not sorry)

| | | |
|---|---|---|
| impenitent | impunity | painful |
| penal | penalize | penalty |
| penance | penitent | penitentiary |
| penology | punish | punishment |
| punitive | repent | |

# Analysis

Choose a word from the Word List to match the literal definition; then create a sentence using the word you chose and the words given.

1. "decide wrongly": _____

   the captive _____

2. "not according to law": _____

   drugs/detain _____

3. "to make no longer a wrongdoing": _____

   marijuana/resistance _____

4. "state of not being hurt": _____

   escape with _____

5. "state of being not fair": _____

   minorities/accept _____

6. "full of hurt": _____

   injury/receive _____

7. "not sorry": _____

   criminal/continue _____

8. "full of fairness": _____

   decision/ponder _____

9. "state of having a court voice": _____

   over the case/insist _____

10. "not according to law": _____

    child/maintain _____

# Relationships

I.  Many of the words on the Word List are commonly used with other words. Choose a word (the root of the word is in parentheses) to go with the following words or phrases.

_____ 1. _____ age, _____ holiday, _____ pad (leg)

_____ 2. _____ court, _____ justice, _____ law (crim)

_____ 3. _____ system, _____ review, _____ branch (jud)

_____ 4. crime and _____, the _____ must fit the crime (pen)

_____ 5. pass _____, the last _____, awarded a _____ (jud)

_____ 6. _____ against women, _____ against minorities (crim)

_____ 7. civil rights _____, _____ of the land (leg)

_____ 8. hung _____, sequestered _____ (jur)

_____ 9. commit _____ on the stand, guilty of _____ (jur)

_____ 10. _____ damage, _____ parents (pen)

_____ 11. _____ code, _____ colony (pen)

II. Complete the following analogies, using words from the Word List.

1. state : _____ :: nation : congress

2. _____ : criminology :: jail : crime

3. proposal : bill :: _____ : law

4. jail : city :: _____ : state

5. counselor : resolve :: judge : _____

6. appointed : judge :: elected : _____

7. pastor : marriage :: _____ : divorce

8. _____ : referee :: fine : judge

9. basketball : foul :: football : _____

10. _____ : thought :: discrimination : action

# Collaborative Work

Answer the following questions or work the problems alone, and then discuss your answers in a group.

1. What are the most **criminogenic** factors or conditions in your native country?

   _____

   _____

2. In some religions, people are asked to **repent** their sins and be **penitent** for their wrongdoings. Then they are asked to do **penance**. In simpler English, what does this mean?

   _____

   _____

3. What is **incriminating** evidence?

   _____

4. What is **legalese**? Write a sentence in **legalese**.

   _____

   _____

5. Do you think a country can **legislate** morality?

   _____

217

# 32 Roots of Law and Society II

The following roots describe those qualities any society needs to have if it is to function well; we need truth, certainty, trust, and a sense of right and wrong.

## WORD LIST

**ver: true, truth; to prove**

**Example:** What is the **verdict** of the jury? (a truthful saying)

| | | |
|---|---|---|
| aver | veracious | veracity |
| verdict | verification | verify |
| verisimilitude | verity | |

**cert (cern): to be sure, figure out, approve, prove**

**Example:** We must **ascertain** the problem. (to figure out)

| | | |
|---|---|---|
| ascertain | certain | certainly |
| certainty | certificate | certification |
| certify | certitude | decertify |
| discern | | |

**fid (fed): to trust, have faith, pledge; a group that trusts**

**Example:** I **confide** in my lawyer. ([speak] with total trust)

| | | |
|---|---|---|
| confederacy | confidant | confide |
| confident | diffident | federal |
| federate | fidelity | infidel |
| infidelity | | |

**rect (right): straight, proper, right**

**Example:** This is a **direct** flight. (straight)

| | | |
|---|---|---|
| correct | direct | erect |
| incorrigible | rectangle | rectifiable |
| rectify | rectitude | righteousness |

# Analysis

Analyze and give the literal definition for each of the following terms. Use the sentence to help you form the definition.

1. certify: _____

   The judge **certified** the results of the election.

2. verify: _____

   Could you please **verify** the amount of money in my account, so I can make the required adjustments?

3. correct: _____

   Are you certain that is the **correct** amount?

4. confide: _____

   I need to **confide** in my judicious friend.

5. confidant: _____

   She is both my friend and **confidant**.

6. certitude: _____

   I can say, with complete **certitude**, that the sun will rise tomorrow.

7. verity: _____

   "All humans are mortal" is an eternal **verity**.

8. certainty: _____

   The jurors came to their verdict with absolute **certainty** and confidence.

9. federate: _____

   The independent republics began to **federate**.

10. certification: _____

    She has a **certification** to teach math, science, and music.

# Relationships

Complete the following analogies, using words from the Word List.

1. falsehood : lie :: _____ : truth

2. build up : _____ :: tear down : raze

3. introvert : extrovert :: diffident : _____

4. love : marriage :: _____ : divorce

5. atheist : _____ :: believer : follower

6. four : eight :: _____ : octagon

7. _____ : mendacious :: truth : lie

8. jury : _____ :: judge : sentence

9. North : South :: Union : _____

10. city : county :: state : _____

11. birth : _____ :: graduation : diploma

# Collaborative Work

Answer the following questions alone and then discuss them in a group.

1. Why would a bank include the word **fidelity** in its name, as in "Fidelity Mutual Savings Bank"?

   _____

2. Are irrevocable mistakes **rectifiable**? Why or why not?

   _____

   _____

3. What are the qualities of an **incorrigible** child? How might the child be **directed** to change?

   _____

   _____

4. What is moral **rectitude** or moral **righteousness**?

_____

_____

5. In general, which has more **verisimilitude**, a photograph or a drawing? Why?

_____

_____

6. Explain the differences among the following phrases or sentences:

**Aver** the truth.

_____

**Ascertain** the truth.

_____

**Discern** the truth.

_____

**Verify** the truth.

_____

7. What does it mean to **decertify** a union or an individual?

_____

# 33 Roots of Law and Society III

People, people everywhere. The roots dealing with people and the groups they form are used in many words in the language.

## WORD LIST

<u>soc</u>: group, groups of people, companions

**Example:**    I need a **social** science class. (related to groups)

| | | |
|---|---|---|
| antisocial | associate | association |
| dissociate | sociable | social |
| socialist | socialite | socialize |
| society | sociologist | sociopath |

<u>pop</u> (<u>pub</u>): people, groups

**Example:**    This is **public** information. ([known] to people)

| | | |
|---|---|---|
| depopulate | pop | populace |
| popular | popularize | populate |
| population | populist | populous |
| public | publicist | publicize |
| publish | republic | |

<u>polis</u>: city, government

**Example:**    In Athens, visit the **Acropolis.** (high city)

| | | |
|---|---|---|
| Acropolis | cosmopolitan | megalopolis |
| metropolitan | necropolis | police |
| policy | political | politician |
| politics | | |

demo: people

**Example:** They made **democratic** reforms. (related to rule by people)

demagogue      democracy      democratic
democratize      demographer      demographics
epidemic      pandemic

civ (cit): city, government, one who lives in the city

**Example:** She is a **citizen** of Tokyo. (one who lives in the city)

citadel      citizen      citizenship
city      civic      civil
civilian      civility      civilization
civilize

# Analysis

Analyze and give a literal definition for each of the boldface terms. Then write a sentence using the given phrase.

1. incorrigible **antisocial** behavior

_____

_____

2. **popular** show

_____

_____

3. confident **politician**

_____

_____

4. **pandemic** fear

_____

_____

5. **civic** pride

_____

_____

6. **sociable** person

_____

_____

7. **populous** city

_____

_____

8. American **democracy**

_____

_____

9. **civilize** the people

_____

_____

10. **citizenship** test

_____

_____

11. **epidemic** disease

_____

_____

12. New York **megalopolis**

_____

_____

**13. publicize** the verdict

_____

_____

**14. popularize** opera

_____

_____

**15. socialize** at the party

_____

_____

# Relationships

I. Choose the word from the Word List that is commonly used in the following instances. Define each new phrase.

_____ 1. _____ war, _____ disobedience, _____ rights

_____

_____

_____ 2. _____ party, _____ government, _____ movement

_____

_____

_____ 3. _____ dog, _____ officer, _____ state

_____

_____

_____ 4. _____ art, _____ music, _____ culture

_____

_____

_____ 5. _____ disease, _____ science, _____ security

_____

_____

_____ 6. _____ hall, _____ council, _____ editor

_____

_____

_____ 7. _____ science, _____ terrorism, _____ party

_____

_____

_____ 8. _____ assistance, _____ health, _____ school

_____

_____

_____ 9. _____ explosion, _____ control, _____ figures

_____

_____

_____ 10. fiscal _____, public _____, monetary _____

_____

_____

II. There are many people and professions on the Word List. Match the people to their interests or "job description."

_____ 1. socialist     A. groups, conflict, social change, families

_____ 2. socialite     B. newspapers, magazines, books

_____ 3. sociologist     C. government, laws, elections, power, committees

_____ 4. publicist     D. parties, dinners, concerts, dances

_____ 5. populist     E. life outside the military

_____ 6. politician     F. "grassroots" democracy, public opinion

_____ 7. demographer   G. leading people for his or her own gain

_____ 8. demagogue     H. strong central government with many public services

_____ 9. citizen       I. census data, population shifts, income changes

_____ 10. civilian     J. all of the above

# Collaborative Work

Answer the following questions or work the problems alone, and then discuss your answers in groups.

1. Explain the differences among an **association**, a **society**, and a **civilization**.

   _____

   _____

   _____

2. Would you choose to **associate** with or **dissociate** from a **sociopath**? Why?

   _____

   _____

3. In general, are the **republics** of the world **democratizing**? Why or why not?

   _____

   _____

4. In studying the **demographics** of America or your country, are **metropolitan** areas **populating** or **depopulating**? Why?

   _____

   _____

5. What would you expect to find in a **necropolis**, the **Acropolis**, a **citadel**, and a **cosmopolitan** city?

   _____

   _____

   _____

# 34 Roots of Law and Society IV

Every social group must have a system of control or some type of government if it is to function. Thus, many words in the language connect to these various rules, regulations, and governments.

## WORD LIST

**reg (roy): to rule, control, govern; kings and queens**

**Example:** The **royal** banners flew. (related to king and queen)

| | | |
|---|---|---|
| deregulate | misrule | realm |
| regal | regent | regicide |
| regime | region | regulate |
| regulation | regulator | reign |
| royal | royalty | ruler |

**dom: to rule, control, govern; a house**

**Example:** There is **domestic** violence. (related to the house)

| | | |
|---|---|---|
| condominium | despot | domain |
| domestic | domesticated | domicile |
| dominant | dominate | domination |
| domineer | dominion | indomitable |

**liber: to free, set free, remove control**

**Example:** **Deliver** us from evil. (to free from)

| | | |
|---|---|---|
| deliver | liberalize | liberate |
| liberator | libertarian | libertine |
| liberty | | |

**serve**: to save, protect, aid, assist, help

Example:    **Conserve** your strength. (save completely)

| | | |
|---|---|---|
| conserve | disservice | observe |
| preserve | reserve | serf |
| servant | serve | servile |
| servitude | subservient | |

---

**vict** (**vinc**, **vanq**): conquer, defeat, beat, overpower

Example:    You have **convinced** me. (overpowered my mind)

| | | |
|---|---|---|
| convict | conviction | convince |
| evict | invincible | province |
| vanquish | victim | victor |
| victory | | |

---

**arch**: first, most important, first ruler; rule

Example:    The culture is a **matriarchy**. (ruled by mothers)

| | | |
|---|---|---|
| anarchist | anarchy | archaeologist |
| archangel | archbishop | architect |
| archrival | autocracy | matriarch |
| monarch | oligarchy | patriarch |

# Analysis

Give a literal definition for the boldface terms in the following sentences.

1. The airlines have been **deregulated**.

   _____

2. The citadel-like **royal** mansion covered two city blocks.

   _____

3. **Domestic** violence has increased dramatically in metropolitan areas.

   _____

4. Her **indomitable** spirit against political oppression gave courage to us all.

   _____

5. Her **invincible** pride caused her insurmountable problems.

   _____

6. To promote the social good, the company **liberalized** rules for maternity leave.

   _____

7. The demagogue, for great **disservice** to his fellow citizens, was severely criticized in the popular press.

   _____

8. For three years, Harvard lost to its **archrival**, Yale.

   _____

9. You cannot **convince** me to change my mind on this domestic policy.

   _____

10. Food, clothing, and shelter are the **dominant** needs in any civilization.

    _____

# Relationships

**I.** Complete the following analogies, using words from the Word List.

1. tyrant : liberator :: oppress : _____

2. dominant : leader :: _____ : follower

3. Canada : _____ :: America : state

4. _____ : tenant :: expel : student

5. _____ : dog :: wild : wolf

6. residence : _____ :: house : home

7. term : president :: _____ : king

8. one : autocracy :: few : _____

9. apartment : rent :: _____ : own

10. laws : govern :: rules : _____

II. There are a number of people and professions on the Word List. Match the people to who they are or what they do.

_____ 1. someone completely controlled by society; an inmate

_____ 2. someone who believes in complete individual freedom from government

_____ 3. someone who believes there should be no government

_____ 4. a winner; a conqueror

_____ 5. one who rules or governs a college

_____ 6. a king or queen

_____ 7. kings, queens, princes, dukes, duchesses

_____ 8. someone hurt by a criminal

_____ 9. an important leader in the church

_____ 10. one who insures that rules are followed

_____ 11. a leader of any country

_____ 12. a harsh, evil ruler

_____ 13. a slave

_____ 14. one who frees people

_____ 15. a female head of a family

_____ 16. a male head of a family

_____ 17. one who studies early civilizations

_____ 18. one who is free with money and pleasure

_____ 19. one who helps others

_____ 20. one who first plans a building or policy

III. Delete the term that does not fit with the others and give a general category name to the rest.

1. realm   region   domain   dominion   liberty

   Category: _____

2. vanquish   domineer   dominate

   Category: _____

3. observe   reserve   conserve   preserve

   Category: _____

# Collaborative Work

Rewrite the following sentences in simpler English. Do this alone and then compare sentences in groups.

1. Under the evil **regime**, the populace was **subservient** to the **royal despot's misrule**.

   _____

   _____

2. The years of **servitude** ended with a **regicide**.

   _____

   _____

3. After the criminal **convictions** of all the **royalty**, **anarchy** was pandemic and society was threatened.

   _____

   _____

4. Shortly after this **victory**, the country was under the **domination** of equally poor demagogic **rulers**.

   _____

   _____

5. Eventually, true **liberty** was instituted, **regulations** were democratically created, and the government **served** the people and **preserved** their hard-won political and social freedom.

_____

_____

_____

# Review V

Give the meaning of the root; then analyze the boldfaced term and write its literal definition.

## Unit 24  Roots of the Senses I

| Root | Meaning | Phrase | Literal Definition |
|------|---------|--------|--------------------|
| voc | _____ | a **vociferous** crowd | _____ |
| dict | _____ | **dictate** policy | _____ |
| claim | _____ | **reclaim** freedoms | _____ |
| log | _____ | clamorous **dialogue** | _____ |
| chor | _____ | the **chorus** line | _____ |

## Unit 25  Roots of the Senses II

| spect | _____ | **prospect** for gold | _____ |
| vid | _____ | **video** games | _____ |
| aud | _____ | a captive **audience** | _____ |
| phon | _____ | a Mozart **symphony** | _____ |
| tang | _____ | a **tangled** mess | _____ |

## Unit 26  Roots of Life Processes I

| bio | _____ | take **antibiotics** | _____ |
| viv | _____ | **survive** the storm | _____ |
| nat | _____ | love of **nature** | _____ |
| gen | _____ | the **gene** for height | _____ |
| gen | _____ | a **genial** friend | _____ |

## Unit 27  Roots of Life Processes II

card  _____  a **cordial** welcome  _____

corp  _____  a huge **corporation**  _____

path  _____  a **passion** for life  _____

sens  _____  a **senseless** crime  _____

## Unit 28  Roots of Mental Activity

ment  _____  a **demented** criminal  _____

cred  _____  an opposing **creed**  _____

mnes  _____  grant **amnesty**  _____

gnos  _____  **diagnose** problems  _____

qui  _____  take a **quiz**  _____

doc  _____  **doctrine** of peace  _____

lec  _____  **select** an answer  _____

## Unit 29  Roots of Qualities

fort  _____  **enforce** the law  _____

clar  _____  **clarify** the issue  _____

dur  _____  **durable** goods  _____

grat  _____  **gracious** hosts  _____

sat  _____  **satisfy** the need  _____

val  _____  **valuable** lesson  _____

## Unit 30  Abstract Roots

pend  _____  **impending** storm  _____

| stat | _____ | **constant** speed | _____ |
| ceive | _____ | **conceive** a child | _____ |
| tain | _____ | **maintain** support | _____ |
| sign | _____ | **sign** of the times | _____ |

## Unit 31  Roots of Law and Society I

| jus | _____ | **justice** for all | _____ |
| leg | _____ | equal before the **law** | _____ |
| crim | _____ | **criminal** justice | _____ |
| pen | _____ | severe **penalty** | _____ |

## Unit 32  Roots of Law and Society II

| ver | _____ | **veracious** woman | _____ |
| cert | _____ | birth **certificate** | _____ |
| fed | _____ | **federal** government | _____ |
| rect | _____ | **erect** a monument | _____ |

## Unit 33  Roots of Law and Society III

| soc | _____ | **social** problems | _____ |
| pop | _____ | **popular** actor | _____ |
| polis | _____ | city **police** | _____ |
| demo | _____ | **democratic** reforms | _____ |
| civ | _____ | **civil** disobedience | _____ |

## Unit 34  Roots of Law and Society IV

| reg | _____ | **regulate** the peace | _____ |

| | | | |
|---|---|---|---|
| <u>dom</u> | _____ | **domesticated** cat | _____ |
| <u>liber</u> | _____ | **liberate** the people | _____ |
| <u>serve</u> | _____ | **serve** the people | _____ |
| <u>vict</u> | _____ | criminal **conviction** | _____ |
| <u>arch</u> | _____ | demented **anarchist** | _____ |

# Review V: Reading

## The Sweep Toward Democracy

In recent decades, the world has seen a new group of <u>popular</u> and <u>valiant</u> heroes. Lech Walesa in Poland, Corazon Aquino in the Philippines, Raul Alfonsin in Argentina, Nelson Mandela in South Africa, and students in China are but a few examples of men and women who have shown the world a <u>fortitude</u> of spirit and a <u>passion</u> for free-

experienced the genesis of democratization.

In many nations human beings proclaim their rights before obdurate dictators. There are also social and political forces that can break even the most repressive, punitive governments. Ironically, the first force for change is the aging despots and authorities themselves. Some rulers consider themselves invincible and simply ignore or despise the dissenting voices of those who advocate reform. Others tenaciously cling to their power and persist in efforts to preserve their position. Other leaders, forced by discord to grant some free elections or a few civil liberties or human rights, find themselves faced with a growing, confident chorus, demanding a greater say in domestic policy and legislation. And soon, once seemingly indomitable rulers can no longer survive, for people recognize what they want and are willing to work tirelessly to attain their goals.

This growing capacity of people to know what they want is the second force behind the international movement toward democracy. People all over the world no longer live in ignorance of or isolation from richer, freer people. Magazines, radios, and television now offer their audiences clear pictures, sounds, and words of how liberal, democratic republics work. How can some citizens accept injustice when they see others free from misrule? When memorable, vivid events occur, such as the fall of the Berlin Wall or the riots in Tiananmen Square, the entire world can see instantly the spirit of freedom through these media.

People of the world can also see and know that Western Europe, the United States, Japan, Canada, and other strong democracies manufacture many consumer goods and maintain strong economies. These plentiful goods and the high standards of living in such democracies are reminders to poorer or less free societies that free governments encourage free markets. Thus, the contagious desire to move toward

dom. These and many others have endured great discomfort and overcome enormous obstacles to institute democratic movements in their countries. In every region of the world, there is a clamor for change and an insistence on liberal reforms.

Freedom House, an American research association, recently ascertained that of the 171 countries of the world, there are 89 full democracies and 32 nations in quest of greater liberty. In 1972, by contrast, there were but 44 democracies. In 1982, 44% of the world's population was judged to be "not free" and dominated in repressive regimes. Ten years later, only 32% continued in such discouraging circumstances. In a mere decade, over 1.2 billion people in such widely scattered countries as Thailand, Nigeria, El Salvador, Poland, and South Africa democracy is _engendered_ by the knowledge of how _comfortable_ and free other people of the world have become.

Unfortunately, the desire to be free and the _courageous_ efforts of women and men will not guarantee that democracy will take hold and grow in a nation. To _vanquish_ an _apathetic_ old government and to create and _sustain_ a new one with _vitality_ is no easy task for inexperienced new leaders. A young nation may have domestic _politics degenerate_ into _anarchy_ or a _police_ state. Furthermore, _demagogues_ who may be potentially worse than the overthrown _dictators_, _discredit_ the _efforts_ of the new leaders in hopes of solidifying their own power. So even the most _valiant_ efforts by reformers may come to nothing, for the tender life of a new democracy is always _uncertain_.

Despite the _incredible_ problems and dangers, people always have sought and _consistently_ will seek greater personal, political, economic, _legal_, and social freedoms. Today, the best available choice to _obtain_ those goals is _liberal_ democracy. Of the 171 nations of the world, 121 are clearly moving in that direction. This is an unmistakable _signal_ to the remaining fifty countries, and perhaps your children will see a world in which all 171 nations have created governments that _serve_ the people and _constitutions_ that _irrevocably_ grant _valuable_ and _durable_ freedoms to their societies.

## Questions

1. Return to the text and circle any underlined terms that you don't know. Try to analyze and form a literal definition for these terms by using the Glossary. If you still cannot form a clear definition, have a member of your group help you.
2. Write a short essay in which you trace the historical movement toward liberal reform or democracy within your native country.
3. Look back to the word lists in Units 24–34. Using at least twenty words from the lists, write a short essay on one of the following topics:

   a. Disease

   b. Reproduction

   c. Memory

   d. Crime and Punishment

# Glossary of Roots and Affixes Used in the Text

This section contains most of the prefixes, suffixes, and roots used in *Developing Vocabulary Skills*. (If the root of a word is also a word by itself, it is probably not included here.)

If you do not find the exact word part, look for word elements that resemble the spelling. Many word parts in English have a variety of different forms, so don't give up your search quickly. In addition, a word element can sometimes have two meanings, as in <u>ped</u> and <u>ped</u> or <u>man</u> and <u>man.</u> Be sure you have the right one before you make a judgment on the meaning of the word. Finally, you will find that many of the example words also appear in the text.

A hypen (-) following an element indicates a prefix; a hyphen preceding an element indicates a suffix; all other entries are roots. A brief etymology is provided for each root and for certain affixes. This indicates the language from which the term was borrowed, the word in that language from which the root was formed, and a short definition of the word in the original language.

Abbreviations used:

| | | | |
|---|---|---|---|
| E. | English | Gr. | Greek | ME. | Middle English |
| Fr. | French | L. | Latin | OE. | Old English |
| Frk. | Frankish | | | | |

| Word Element | Meaning | Etymology | Examples |
|---|---|---|---|

# A

| Word Element | Meaning | Etymology | Examples |
|---|---|---|---|
| **a-** | without | | apolitical, amoral |
| **ab-** | away, away from | | absent, abnormal |
| **-able** | can do something | | readable, likable |
| **academ** | school | *Gr. akademia:* Plato's school | academy, academic |
| **acc-** | to, toward. *See* **ad-** | | accede, accept |
| **acid** | sharp, sour | *L. acidus:* sharp | acidic, antacid |
| **acro-** | height | *Gr. akros:* top | acropolis, acrobat |
| **act** | do something | *L. actum:* something done | enact, action |
| **act** | move. *See* **ad-** | | exact, inexactitude |
| **-acy** | state of being | | primacy, democracy |
| **ad-** | to, toward | | advance, adhere |
| **aff-** | to, toward. *See* **ad-** | | affix, affluent |
| **ag** | force, move | *L. agere:* drive | agitate, agent |
| **-age** | state of being | | marriage, leverage |
| **agg-** | to, toward. *See* **ad-** | | aggression, aggravate |
| **agog** | lead | *Gr. agein:* lead | synagogue, demagogue |
| **agon** | fight, struggle | *Gr. agonia:* contest | agony, antagonist |
| **-al** | within, related to | | natural, physical |
| **alesc** | grow, develop | *L. alescere:* grow | coalesce, adolescent |
| **algia** | pain | *Gr. algia:* pain | cardialgia, analgesic |
| **ali** | other. *See* **alte** | | alibi, alien |
| **all-** | to, toward. *See* **ad-** | | alleviate, allocate |
| **alte** | change, other | *L. alter:* other | alternate, alternative |
| **alti** | height | *L. altus:* height | altitude, altimeter |
| **am** | to take out | *L. emere:* take | example, sample |
| **am** | love, like | *L. amor:* love | amiable, amorous |
| **ambi** | to walk, go | *L. ambire:* go for votes | ambition, ambitious |
| **ambi-** | both, two ways | | ambivalent, ambidextrous |
| **ambl** | to walk | *L. ambulare:* walk | amble, ambulatory |
| **amphi-** | both, two ways. *See* **ambi-** | | amphibian, amphibious |
| **ample** | enough, enlarge | *L. amplus:* enough | amplify, ample |
| **an-** | without | | anarchy, anhydrous |
| **-ance** | state of being | | attendance, acceptance |
| **-ancy** | state of being | | hesitancy, vacancy |
| **andro** | male, man | *Gr. andro:* man | android, polyandry |
| **anemo** | wind | *Gr. anemos:* wind | anemometer |
| **anima** | spirit, soul | *Gr. animus:* soul | animated, equanimity |

| Word Element | Meaning | Etymology | Examples |
|---|---|---|---|
| **ann** | year | *L.* *annus:* year | annual, anniversary |
| **-ant** | one who | | confidant, celebrant |
| **-ant** | related to | | dominant, vacant |
| **ante-** | before | | antecedent, anteroom |
| **anthro** | human | *Gr.* *anthropos:* man | anthropology |
| **anti-** | against | | antacid, antiwar |
| **api** | bee | *L.* *apis:* bee | apiary |
| **app-** | to, toward. *See* **ad-** | | approach, append |
| **apt** | fit, proper | *L.* *aptus:* fit | adapt, inept |
| **aqua** | water | *L.* *aqua:* water | aquatic, aquarium |
| **-ar** | one who, something that | | liar, burglar |
| **-ar** | related to | | regular, perpendicular |
| **arch** | first, head | *Gr.* *arkhos:* head | monarch, archbishop |
| **archy** | rule, government | *Gr.* *arkhein:* rule | monarchy, anarchy |
| **-arian** | one who | | librarian, humanitarian |
| **-arium** | place where, room | | aquarium, planetarium |
| **arm** | weapon | *L.* *arma:* weapon | armory, disarmament |
| **arr-** | to, toward. *See* **ad-** | | arrange, arrive |
| **art** | art, skill | *L.* *ars:* art | artifact |
| **-ary** | a place where | | library, granary |
| **-ary** | related to | | primary, secondary |
| **ass-** | to, toward. *See* **ad-** | | assemble, assimilate |
| **astro** | star | *Gr.* *astron:* star | astronomy, astronaut |
| **-ate** | to make | | elongate, regulate |
| **-ate** | one who | | primate, delegate |
| **-ate** | related to | | accurate, passionate |
| **athl** | sport, game | *Gr.* *athlon:* prize, valor | athletic, pentathlon |
| **atmo** | air, vapor | *Gr.* *atmos:* vapor | atmosphere |
| **att-** | to, toward. *See* **ad-** | | attach, attract |
| **aud** | hear | *L.* *audire:* hear | audio, audition |
| **auto** | self | *Gr.* *autos:* self | automatic, automobile |
| **avis** | bird | *L.* *avis:* bird | aviary, aviation |

# B

| Word Element | Meaning | Etymology | Examples |
|---|---|---|---|
| **bapt** | dip in water | *Gr.* *baptein:* dip | baptize, baptism |
| **baro** | pressure | *Gr.* *baros:* weight | barometer, isobar |
| **bat** | fight | *L.* *battuere:* beat | combat, battle |
| **bel** | sound | *E.* Alexander Graham Bell | decibel |

| Word Element | Meaning | Etymology | Examples |
|---|---|---|---|
| **bell** | war | *L. bellum:* war | antebellum, bellicose |
| **bene** | good | *L. bene:* well | benefit, benefactor |
| **bi-** | two | *L. bis:* two | bicycle, bilateral |
| **biblio** | book | *Gr. biblios:* book | bibliography, biblical |
| **bio** | life | *Gr. bios:* life | biology, biography |
| **botan** | plant | *Gr. botane:* plant | botany, botanist |
| **brev, brid** | short | *L. brevis:* short | brevity, abridge |
| **burgl** | steal | *L. burg:* town | burglar |

# C

| Word Element | Meaning | Etymology | Examples |
|---|---|---|---|
| **caco-** | bad | *Gr. kakos:* bad | cacophony |
| **cad** | happen | *L. cadere:* fall | decadent, cadence |
| **-cade** | parade | | motorcade, aquacade |
| **cam** | room, house | *L. camera:* room | bicameral, camera |
| **cap** | chief, head | *L. captus:* head | captain, capital |
| **cap** | get, receive | *L. capere:* seize | capture, captive |
| **card** | heart, core | *Gr. kardia:* heart | cardiology |
| **carto** | map | *L. carta:* paper | cartography |
| **cast** | throw | *OE. casten:* throw | forecast, broadcast |
| **caut** | care, careful | *L. cavere:* beware | caution, precautions |
| **cede, ceed** | move, yield | *L. cedere:* go, withdraw | proceed, concede |
| **ceive** | get, receive. *See* **cap** | | deceive, conceive |
| **celer** | speed | *L. celer:* swift | decelerate, accelerate |
| **cent** | hundred | *L. centum:* hundred | century, percent |
| **centr** | middle | *L. centrum:* center | central, decentralize |
| **cep** | get, receive. *See* **cap** | | accept, reception |
| **cern** | separate, decide | *L. cernare:* separate | discern, concern |
| **cert** | be true, sure | *L. certus:* certain | certify, certainly |
| **cert** | blend, mingle | *L. cernare:* sift | concerto |
| **cess** | move. *See* **cede** | | process, succession |
| **chie** | head. *See* **cap** | | chief, achieve |
| **chor** | sing, dance | *Gr. khoros:* dance | chorus, choreograph |
| **chrom** | color | *Gr. khroma:* color | chromatic, chromosome |
| **chron** | time | *Gr. khronos:* time | chronic, chronicle |
| **-cian** | one who | | physician, electrician |
| **cide** | kill | *L. caedere:* kill, cut | homicide, pesticide |
| **cide** | to happen. *See* **cad** | | accident, incident |
| **cip** | get, receive. *See* **cap** | | recipient |

| Word Element | Meaning | Etymology | | Examples |
|---|---|---|---|---|
| **circul, circum** | around | *L.* | *circum:* around | circumstance |
| **cise** | cut | *L.* | *caedere:* kill, cut | excise, incision |
| **cit** | town, people | *Gr.* | *civis:* citizen | city, citizen |
| **cite** | move | *L.* | *cire:* call, move | excite, incite |
| **civ** | town, people. *See* **cit** | | | civil, civilian |
| **claim, clam** | talk, shout | *L.* | *clamare:* call | proclaim, exclaim |
| **clar** | clear | *L.* | *clarus:* clear | clarify, clarity |
| **clar, clat** | call | *L.* | *clarere:* call | declare, nomenclature |
| **clen, cline** | bend, lean | *L.* | *clinare:* bend | decline, incline |
| **clos, clud, clus** | close | *L.* | *claudere:* close | closet, recluse, exclude |
| **co-, coll-, com-, con-, corr-** | together, totally, with | | | complete, contact, copilot |
| **commun** | share | *L.* | *commun:* common | communicate, community |
| **consul** | advise | *L.* | *consulere:* advise | consult, counselor |
| **contra-** | against | *L.* | *contra:* opposite | contrary, contradict |
| **cord** | agree, core. *See* **card** | | | cordial, discord |
| **corp** | body | *L.* | *corpus:* body | corporal, corporation |
| **corr-** | *See* **co-** | | | correct, corrupt |
| **cosmo** | world, universe | *Gr.* | *kosmos:* universe | microcosm, cosmopolitan |
| **counter-** | against. *See* **contra** | | | encounter, counterfeit |
| **cour** | run. *See* **cur** | | | courier, course |
| **cour** | heart, soul. *See* **card** | | | encourage, discourage |
| **cracy, crat** | government, rule | *Gr.* | *kratos:* power | democracy, autocrat |
| **crast** | tomorrow | *L.* | *cras:* tomorrow | procrastinate |
| **crea** | make | *L.* | *creare:* make | create, creation |
| **cred** | believe | *L.* | *credere:* believe | credence, incredible |
| **cres, cret** | grow | *L.* | *crescere:* grow | increase, concrete |
| **cret** | separate, decide. *See* **cern** | | | secret, secretive |
| **crim** | wrongdoing | *L.* | *crimen:* crime | criminal, incriminate |
| **crypto** | secret | *Gr.* | *kruptos:* hidden | cryptogram, cryptography |
| **-cule** | small | *L.* | *cula:* small | molecule, minuscule |

**245**

| Word Element | Meaning | Etymology | Examples |
|---|---|---|---|
| **cult** | growth | *L.*  *cultus:* growth | aquaculture, cultivate |
| **cur** | run, happen | *L.*  *currere:* run | current, recur |
| **cura** | help, care | *L.*  *cura:* care | accurate, curator |
| **-cy** | state of being | | normalcy, advocacy |
| **cycle** | wheel, circle | *Gr. kuklos:* circle | bicycle, recycle |

# D

| | | | |
|---|---|---|---|
| **de-** | down | | decline |
| **de-** | away | | depart |
| **de-** | opposite, reversal | | deplete |
| **de-** | remove | | defoliate |
| **dec** | ten | *L.*  *decem:* ten | decade, decimate |
| **dece** | correct, proper | *L.*  *decere:* fitting | decent, indecency |
| **demo** | people | *Fr. demos:* people | democracy, demography |
| **dent** | tooth | *L.*  *dens:* tooth | dental, dentist |
| **di** | two | *Gr. di:* two, twice | divorce, dioxide |
| **dia-** | through | | diameter, diagonal |
| **dia** | day | *L.*  *dies:* day | diary |
| **dic** | say. *See* **dict** | | abdicate |
| **dicho** | two ways | *Gr. dikha:* two ways | dichotomy |
| **dict** | speak, say | *L.*  *dictare:* say | dictate, predict |
| **diem** | day | *L.*  *dies:* day | per diem, ante meridiem |
| **dis-** | not, remove | | disable, disinfect |
| **div** | holy, sacred | *L.*  *divinus:* foresee | divine, divination |
| **do** | two. *See* **du** | | double |
| **doc, dog** | teach, belief. *See* **dox** | | doctrine, dogma |
| **-dom** | state of being, area | | stardom, kingdom |
| **dom** | rule, govern | *L.*  *dominus:* master | dominate, dominion |
| **don** | give | *L.*  *donare:* give | donor, donate |
| **donna** | woman | *L.*  *domina:* woman | prima donna |
| **dorm** | sleep | *L.*  *dormire:* sleep | dormitory, dormant |
| **dox** | belief, idea | *Gr. doxa:* opinion | orthodox, doxology |
| **du** | two | | dual, duet |
| **duc** | lead | *L.*  *ducere:* lead | conduct, induce |
| **dur** | strong, lasting | *L.*  *durus:* hard | endure, duration |
| **dyn** | power | *Gr. dunamis:* power | dyne, dynamic |
| **dys-** | bad | *Gr. dys:* bad | dyslexia, dystrophy |

| Word Element | Meaning | Etymology | Examples |
|---|---|---|---|
| econom | money, manage | *Gr.* *oikonomia:* household economy | microeconomic |
| -ectomy | removal | *L.* *ex + tomy:* cut out | appendectomy |
| edi | house, built | *L.* *aedes:* house | edifice, edify |
| -ee | one who | | nominee, designee |
| ego | self | *L.* *ego:* I | egoist, egocentric |
| electr | electric | *L.* *electrum:* amber | electrify, electron |
| em | take out | *L.* *emere:* take | exempt, preempt |
| en- | to make | | enlarge, enrage |
| -en | to make | | sadden, brighten |
| -en | made of, related to | | wooden, golden |
| -ence, -ency | state of being | | difference, presidency |
| energ | work, power | *Gr.* *ergon:* work | energize, energetic |
| engin | talent, skill | *L.* *ingenium:* talent | engineer, engine |
| enn | year. *See* **ann** | | perennial, centennial |
| -ent | like. *See* -**ant** | | sentient, lenient |
| epi- | above, throughout | | epidemic, epicenter |
| equa, equi | the same | *L.* *aequus:* equal | equator, equivalent |
| -er | one who, something that | | farmer, teacher |
| err | wander, be wrong | *L.* *errare:* wander | erratic, error |
| -ery | place where | | bakery, bindery |
| esse | need, exist | *L.* *esse:* to be | essence, essential |
| esthe | feel, sense | *Gr.* *aisthesis:* feeling | anesthesia, esthetics |
| ethn | nationality | *Gr.* *ethnos:* people | ethnic, polyethnic |
| etymon | root word | *Gr.* *etymon:* true sense | etymology |
| eu- | good, well | *Gr.* *eus:* good | eugenics, euphonious |
| eva | time, era | *L.* *aevus:* age | medieval, primeval |
| ex- | out, out of | | expel, extract |
| exam | weigh, test | *L.* *examen:* weigh | examine, exam |
| experi | try, test | *L.* *experiri:* test | experiment, experience |
| exter | outside | *L.* *externus:* outward | external, exterior |

| Word Element | Meaning | Etymology | Examples |
|---|---|---|---|
| **F** | | | |
| **fac** | make, do | L. *facere:* make | manufacture, facsimile |
| **face** | form, face | L. *facere:* form | surface, facial |
| **famil** | known | L. *familia:* household | familiar, familiarize |
| **feas, fec** | make. *See* **fic** | | feasible, perfect |
| **fed** | trust, league | L. *foederare:* league | confederate, federal |
| **feit** | make, do. *See* **fac** | | surfeit, counterfeit |
| **fem** | woman | L. *femina:* woman | feminine, female |
| **fend** | strike, push | L. *defendere:* strike | defend, defensive |
| **fer** | carry | L. *ferre:* carry | differ, transfer |
| **ferti** | growth | L. *fertilis:* produce | fertilize, fertility |
| **fest** | celebrate | L. *festus:* feast | festive, feast |
| **fic** | make, do. *See* **fac** | | fiction, simplification |
| **ficia** | top, surface | L. *facies:* face | superficial |
| **fid** | trust, faith | L. *fidere:* trust | confide, fidelity |
| **fin** | end, complete | L. *finire:* limit | finite, finish |
| **fix** | put, place | L. *fixus:* fastened | affix, fixate |
| **flate** | blow, wind | L. *flate:* blow | inflate, deflate |
| **flect, flex** | bend | L. *flectare:* bend | reflect, flexible |
| **flic** | fight | L. *fligare:* strike | conflict, inflict |
| **flo** | flow | OE. *flowan:* flow | flow, flowage |
| **flor** | flower | L. *flora:* flower | floral, multiflorous |
| **flu** | flo | L. *fluere:* flow | fluid, confluence |
| **foc** | center | L. *focus:* hearth | focus, focal |
| **foli** | leaf | L. *folium:* leaf | foliage, defoliate |
| **for** | bore, hole | L. *forare:* drill | perforate |
| **forc** | strong. *See* **fort** | | force, enforce |
| **fore** | front, early | OE. *fore:* front | forecast, forehead |
| **form** | shape | L. *formare:* form | formal, formation |
| **fort** | strength | L. *fortis:* strong | fortify, fortitude |
| **fortun** | luck, chance | L. *fortuna:* by chance | misfortune, fortuitous |
| **fract, frag** | break | L. *fractus:* broken | fracture, fragment |
| **frat** | brother | L. *frater:* brother | fraternity, fratricide |
| **fring** | break. *See* **fract** | | infringe, frangible |
| **fug** | move, run | L. *fugere:* flee | fugitive, centrifugal |
| **-ful** | full of | | helpful, careful |

| Word Element | Meaning | Etymology | | Examples |
|---|---|---|---|---|
| **funct** | purpose, use | *L.* | *functus:* performed | function, malfunction |
| **fus** | join, blend | *L.* | *fusus:* poured together | confuse, fusion |

# G

| Word Element | Meaning | Etymology | | Examples |
|---|---|---|---|---|
| **gage** | promise | *Frk.* | *wadi:* pledge | engage, mortgage |
| **gam** | marriage | *Gr.* | *gamos:* marriage | bigamy, polygamy |
| **gard** | watch. *See* **guard** | | | regard, disregard |
| **gastro** | stomach | *Gr.* | *gaster:* belly | gastric, gastrectomy |
| **geal** | gel, solidify | *L.* | *gelare:* freeze | congeal, gelatin |
| **gen** | race, birth | *L.* | *genus:* birth, race | genus, homogenize |
| **gen** | produce | *L.* | *genus:* birth, race | generate, engender |
| **genu** | knee | *L.* | *genu:* knee | genuflect |
| **geo** | earth | *Gr.* | *ge:* earth | geology, geography |
| **gero** | old, elderly | *Gr.* | *geron:* old man | geriatric, geriatrician |
| **gest** | take in, carry | *L.* | *gerere:* carry | ingest, gestation |
| **giga** | huge, large | *Gr.* | *giga:* giant | gigantic, giant |
| **glac** | ice | *L.* | *glaces:* ice | glacier |
| **glot** | tongue, language | *Gr.* | *glottis:* tongue | polyglot, epiglottis |
| **gnos** | know | *Gr.* | *gnosis:* knowledge | cognition, recognize |
| **gogue** | leader. *See* **agog** | | | demagogue, pedagogue |
| **gon** | angle | *Gr.* | *gonia:* angle | pentagon, polygon |
| **gov** | rule, control | *L.* | *gubernare:* direct | govern, government |
| **grad** | step, move | *L.* | *gradus:* step | grade, gradual |
| **gram** | written, drawn | *Gr.* | *gramma:* letter | telegram, diagram |
| **graph** | written, instrument | *Gr.* | *graphein:* write | telegraph, monograph |
| **graphy** | writings, study | *Gr.* | *graphein:* write | geography, calligraphy |
| **grat** | pleasing, thankful | *L.* | *gratus:* favorable | gratify, ingratitude |
| **grav** | heavy, weighty | *L.* | *gravis:* heavy | gravity, grave |
| **gree** | pleasing. *See* **grat** | | | disagree, agreeable |
| **greg** | flock, gather | *L.* | *grex:* flock, herd | gregarious, egregious |
| **gress** | move. *See* **grad** | | | progress, ingress |
| **guard** | watch, protect | *L.* | *guader:* look at | guard, guardian |

| Word Element | Meaning | Etymology | Examples |
|---|---|---|---|
| **H** | | | |
| **hab** | live | *L. habitare:* reside | habitat, inhabitant |
| **hale** | breathe | *L. halere:* breathe | exhale, halitosis |
| **hap** | occur, chance | *ME. happ:* chance | happen, mishap |
| **haust** | drain | *L. haurire:* pull | exhaust |
| **helio** | sun | *Gr. helios:* sun | heliocentric |
| **hemi-** | half | | hemisphere |
| **hepta** | seven | *Gr. hepta:* seven | heptathlon |
| **herb** | plant | *L. herba:* plant | herbicide, herbivore |
| **here, hes** | stick together | *L. haerere:* cling | cohere, adhesive |
| **hesit** | wait, hold back | *L. haesitare:* stick | hesitate, unhesitant |
| **hetero-** | different | | heteronym, heterosexual |
| **hilar** | laugh, cheer | *Gr. hilarus:* cheer | exhilarate, hilarious |
| **homo-** | same | | homogenize, homosexual |
| **homo** | human | *L. homo:* human | homicide, *ad hominem* |
| **-hood** | state of being | | statehood, childhood |
| **hor** | shake, tremble | *L. horrere:* shake | abhor, horrify |
| **hort** | urge, encourage | *L. hortari:* urge | exhort, hortatory |
| **hum** | human, people | *L. humanis:* human | humanity, humane |
| **hydr** | water, fluid | *Gr. hudor:* water | hydrant, dehydrate |
| **hyper-** | above | | hyperactive, hypertension |
| **hypo** | below | | hypothermia, hypodermic |
| **I** | | | |
| **-ian** | one who | | librarian, guardian |
| **-iatric** | medical treatment | *Gr. iasthai:* cure | pediatrics, geriatric |
| **-ible** | can do | | possible, digestible |
| **-ic** | related to | | volcanic, acidic |
| **ideo** | idea, thought | *Gr. ideo:* idea | ideogram, ideology |
| **-ify** | to make | | certify, magnify |
| **il-** | not | | illegal, illegible |
| **-ile** | like. *See* **-ine** | | fragile, motile |
| **im-** | into | | immigrate, immerse |
| **im-, in-** | not | | impractical, inexact |
| **imag** | likeness, mirror | *L. imago:* image | imagine, image |
| **in-** | inside, into | | inner, interior |
| **incid** | happen | *L. incidere:* happen | incident, coincide |

| Word Element | Meaning | Etymology | | Examples |
|---|---|---|---|---|
| **-ine** | related to | | | saline, feminine |
| **infra-** | lower, beneath | L. | *infra:* below | infrastructure |
| **-ing** | process, action | | | reading, running |
| **integ** | whole, complete | L. | *integere:* whole | integral, disintegrate |
| **intell** | think, mind | L. | *intellectus:* mind | intellect, intelligent |
| **inter-** | between | | | interstate, interview |
| **init** | begin | L. | *initium:* beginning | initial, initiate |
| **intra-** | within | | | intrastate, intramural |
| **intro-** | into | | | introduce, introspective |
| **-ion** | state of being | | | adhesion, procession |
| **ir-** | not | | | irregular, irrational |
| **-ish** | like | | | foolish, childish |
| **-ism** | belief in, state of | | | socialism, alcoholism |
| **-ist** | one who | | | socialist, dentist |
| **-ite** | one who, something that | | | favorite, graphite |
| **-ity** | state of being | | | gravity, humidity |
| **-ive** | related to, causing | | | inventive, digestive |
| **-ize** | to make | | | minimize, centralize |

# J

| Word Element | Meaning | Etymology | | Examples |
|---|---|---|---|---|
| **jac, ject, jet** | throw, be near | L. | *jacere:* throw | eject, adjacent |
| **joi** | join. *See* **junct** | | | joint, conjoin |
| **jour** | day | Fr. | *jour:* day | journal, journey |
| **jud** | rule, law | L. | *judicare:* judge | judge, judicial |
| **junct** | join together | L. | *jungere:* join | junction, conjunction |
| **jur, jus** | law, rule | L. | *justus:* fair, just | jury, justice |
| **juven** | young | L. | *juvenis:* young | juvenile |
| **juxta** | next to. *See* **jac** | | | juxtapose |

# L

| Word Element | Meaning | Etymology | | Examples |
|---|---|---|---|---|
| **lab** | work | L. | *laborare:* work | collaborate, labor |
| **lap** | fall, miss | L. | *lapsus:* sliding | collapse, relapse |
| **lat** | bring, carry | L. | *latus:* carried | translate, correlate |
| **lat** | line | L. | *latus:* line | multilateral, bilateral |

| Word Element | Meaning | Etymology | | Examples |
|---|---|---|---|---|
| **lau, lav** | wash, clean | *L.* | *laver:* wash | laundry, lavatory |
| **law** | law. *See* **leg** | | | lawful, lawyer |
| **lect, leg** | read, choose | *L.* | *legere:* gather, read | collect, legible |
| **leg** | law | *L.* | *legalis:* law | illegal, legislate |
| **-less** | without | | | hopeless, careless |
| **-let** | small, young | | | starlet, piglet |
| **-lev** | lift, improve | *L.* | *levare:* lift | lever, elevate |
| **lex** | read. *See* **lect** | | | dyslexia |
| **liber** | free | *L.* | *liber:* free | liberate, liberal |
| **libra** | book | *L.* | *liber:* book | library, libretto |
| **libra** | balance | *L.* | *libra:* balance | equilibrium |
| **lict** | permit | *L.* | *licere:* allow | illicit, licit |
| **lide** | strike, move | *L.* | *laedere:* strike | collide, elide |
| **liev** | lift, improve. *See* **lev** | | | relieve, believe |
| **lim** | bound, restrict | *L.* | *limes:* boundary | limits, illimitable |
| **lin** | line | *L.* | *linea:* line | linear, rectilinear |
| **ling** | language | *L.* | *lingua:* tongue | linguist, bilingual |
| **lis** | move. *See* **lide** | | | collision |
| **lit** | read, letter, word | *L.* | *littera:* letter | literate, letter |
| **litho** | stone | *Gr.* | *lithos:* stone | monolith, lithograph |
| **loc** | place | *L.* | *locus:* place | locate, dislocation |
| **loc** | speak. *See* **loq** | | | elocution, interlocutor |
| **log, logy** | study, speech | *Gr.* | *logos:* speech, reason | logic, biology |
| **loq, loqu** | speech | *L.* | *loqui:* speak | eloquent, soliloquy |
| **luce** | shine, bright | *L.* | *lucere:* shine | lucent, translucent |
| **lud, lus** | play, act | *L.* | *ludere:* play | collusion, prelude |
| **lust** | bright | *L.* | *lustere:* brighten | illustrate, luster |
| **-ly** | in a way that is. . . | | | carelessly, slowly |
| **lys, lyt** | break up | *L.* | *luein:* loosen | analytic, analysis |

# M

| Word Element | Meaning | Etymology | | Examples |
|---|---|---|---|---|
| **macro** | large, great | *Gr.* | *makros:* great | macrocosm, macroeconomic |
| **magna** | large, great | *L.* | *magnus:* great | magnify, magnanimous |
| **main** | stay, last | *L.* | *manere:* remain | remain, remainder |
| **mal-** | bad, evil, wrong | *L.* | *malus:* bad | malady, malicious |
| **man** | stay, last. *See* **main** | | | permanent |

| Word Element | Meaning | Etymology | Examples |
|---|---|---|---|
| **manu** | hand | *L. manus:* hand | manual, manufacture |
| **mar** | sea | *L. mare:* sea | marine, maritime |
| **mar** | wonder | *L. mirus:* wonder | marvel, marvelous |
| **mat** | ripe, timely | *L. maturas:* ripe | mature, immaturity |
| **mater** | mother | *L. mater:* mother | maternity, maternal |
| **mea** | go through | *L. meare:* pass | permeate, impermeable |
| **mech** | instrument, tool | *Gr. mekhane:* machine | mechanize, mechanical |
| **medi** | middle | *L. medius:* middle | medium, intermediate |
| **medic** | healing | *L. medicus:* doctor | medical, medicate |
| **mega** | large, great | *Gr. megas:* great | megaton, megahertz |
| **melli-** | sweet, pleasant | *L. mel:* honey | mellifluous |
| **mem** | mind, memory | *L. memoria:* memory | remember, memoir |
| **mence** | begin. *See* **init** | | commence, commencement |
| **mense** | month | *L. mensis:* month | month, menstruate |
| **ment** | mind | *L. mens:* mind | mental, mentality |
| **-ment** | state of being | | argument, placement |
| **merch** | trade, sell | *L. merx:* trade | merchant, merchandise |
| **meri** | middle. *See* **medi** | | meridiem |
| **merg, mers** | mix, enter | *L. mergere:* plunge | immerse, emerge |
| **mest** | month. *See* **mense** | | semester, trimester |
| **meteor** | atmosphere | *Gr. meteoron:* high in the air | meteorology |
| **meter** | measure | *Gr. metron:* measure | speedometer, micrometer |
| **metro** | home, central point | *Gr. meter:* mother | metropolis, metrocenter |
| **metry** | study, measurement | *Gr. metron:* measure | geometry, trigonometry |
| **micro** | small | *Gr. mikros:* small | micron, microscope |
| **mid** | center. *See* **medi** | | midday, midpoint |
| **migra** | move to a new place | *L. migrare:* migrate | migrate, immigrate |
| **milit** | army | *L. miles:* soldier | demilitarize, militia |
| **mill** | thousand | *L. mille:* thousand | millimeter, million |
| **min** | small, tiny | *L. minimus:* least | minimum, diminish |
| **min** | stick out | *L. minere:* project | prominent, eminent |
| **mind** | mind, thinking | *OE. gmynd:* mind | mindful, mindless |
| **minis** | help, serve | *L. ministare:* serve | minister, administer |
| **mir** | wonderful | *L. mirus:* wonderful | miracle, admire |

| Word Element | Meaning | Etymology | | Examples |
|---|---|---|---|---|
| **mis-** | wrong | | | misspell, misplace |
| **misc** | mix | *L.* | *miscere:* mix | miscellaneous, miscible |
| **mis, mit** | send | *L.* | *mittere:* send | permission, remit |
| **mnes** | mind, memory | *Gr.* | *mnemon:* mindful | mnemonic, amnesia |
| **mob** | move. *See* **mov** | | | mobile, immobility |
| **mod** | limit, change | *L.* | *modus:* measure | modify |
| **mol** | build, create | *L.* | *molire:* build | demolish, molecule |
| **mon** | warn, tell | *L.* | *monere:* warn | monitor, premonition |
| **mono** | one | *Gr.* | *monos:* single | monotone, monograph |
| **-mony** | state of being | | | matrimony, sanctimony |
| **mor** | custom, proper | *L.* | *mores:* custom | moral, immorality |
| **morph** | form, style | *Gr.* | *morphe:* form | amorphous, morphology |
| **mors, mort** | death | *L.* | *mors:* death | mortify, mortician |
| **mot** | move. *See* **mov** | | | motile, motion |
| **moun** | hill, mountain | *L.* | *mons:* mountain | surmount, mountainous |
| **mov** | move | *L.* | *movere:* move | movement, movable |
| **multi** | many | *L.* | *multus:* much | multiply, multitude |
| **myst** | secret, strange | *L.* | *muein:* keep secret | mystify, mysterious |

# N

| Word Element | Meaning | Etymology | | Examples |
|---|---|---|---|---|
| **nas** | nose | *L.* | *nasus:* nose | nasal, postnasal |
| **nat** | birth, nature | *L.* | *natilis:* born | natal, nativity |
| **naut** | traveler | *Gr.* | *naute:* sailor | astronaut, aquanaut |
| **navi** | sail | *L.* | *navis:* ship | navigate, navy |
| **nec** | tie, bind | *L.* | *nectare:* bind | connect, disconnect |
| **necro** | death | *Gr.* | *nekro:* dead | necropolis |
| **-nee** | one who | | | nominee, designee |
| **neg** | nothing, deny | *L.* | *negare:* deny | negation, negative |
| **neo** | new | *Gr.* | *neos:* new | neologism, neonate |
| **nesia** | island | *Gr.* | *nesos:* island | Polynesia, Micronesia |
| **-ness** | state of being | | | hardness, happiness |
| **neuro** | nerves | *Gr.* | *neuron:* nerve | neurology, neuropathy |
| **noc** | night. *See* **nox** | | | nocturne, nocturnal |
| **nom** | name | *L.* | *nomen:* name | nominate, nomenclature |
| **non-** | not | | | nonstop, nonessential |

| Word Element | Meaning | Etymology | | Examples |
|---|---|---|---|---|
| **norm** | mid, typical | *L.* | *norma:* carpenter's square | norm, abnormal |
| **nounce** | call, say | *L.* | *nuntiare:* announce | denounce, renounce |
| **nov** | new | *L.* | *novus:* new | novel, novice |
| **nox** | night | *L.* | *nox:* night | equinox |
| **null** | none | *L.* | *nullus:* not one | nullify, annul |
| **nunc** | call, say. *See* **nounce** | | | enunciate, denunciation |
| **nupt** | marry | *L.* | *nupta:* wed | prenuptial |
| **nutri** | food | *L.* | *nutrire:* feed | nutrition, nutrients |
| **nym** | name. *See* **nom** | | | synonym, antonym |

# O

| Word Element | Meaning | Etymology | | Examples |
|---|---|---|---|---|
| **ob-, op-** | toward, against | | | obstruct, opponent |
| **octo** | eight | *L.* | *octo:* eight | octopus, octagon |
| **ocul** | eye | *L.* | *oculis:* eye | oculist, binocular |
| **offic** | duty, job | *L.* | *officium:* duty | official, officer |
| **-oid** | in the shape of | | | humanoid, spheroid |
| **olig** | few | *Gr.* | *oligos:* few | oligarchy |
| **-ology** | study of | *Gr.* | *logos:* speech, reason | psychology, geology |
| **omni-** | all | *Gr.* | *omnis:* all | omnipotent, omnivorous |
| **-onomy** | study of | *Gr.* | *onoma:* name | astronomy |
| **oper** | work | *L.* | *opus:* work | operate, opus |
| **opt** | choose | *L.* | *optio:* choice | option, adopt |
| **opti** | sight | *Gr.* | *optos:* light | optician, optical |
| **-or** | one who, something that | | | governor, monitor |
| **ord** | order, fit | *L.* | *ordo:* order | subordinate, ordinal |
| **orga** | tool, whole | *L.* | *organum:* instrument | organize, organ |
| **orig** | begin | *L.* | *origio:* rise | originate, abort |
| **-orium** | a place where. *See* **arium** | | | auditorium, emporium |
| **ornitho** | bird | *Gr.* | *ornis:* bird | ornithology |
| **ortho** | straight, correct | *Gr.* | *orthos:* straight | orthodox, orthography |
| **-ory** | a place where | | | armory, laboratory |
| **-ory** | related to | | | migratory, explanatory |
| **-ous** | full of | | | famous, dangerous |
| **out-** | higher | | | outlive, outrun |
| **over-** | higher | | | overpriced, overbid |

| Word Element | Meaning | Etymology | | Examples |
|---|---|---|---|---|

## P

| Word Element | Meaning | Etymology | | Examples |
|---|---|---|---|---|
| **pac** | peace | *L.* | *pax:* peace | pacifist, Pacific |
| **pact** | fasten together | *L.* | *pangere:* fasten | compact, impacted |
| **pan-** | all | | | Pan-American |
| **pand** | get larger | *L.* | *pandere:* spread | expand, expansion |
| **par** | equal | *L.* | *par:* equal | compare, parity |
| **para** | beyond, abnormal | *Gr.* | *para:* beside | paradox, paranormal |
| **pare** | get ready | *L.* | *parare:* get ready | prepare, separate |
| **pare** | show | *L.* | *parere:* show | transparent |
| **part** | equal, segment | *L.* | *pars:* equal | partial, partisan |
| **pater** | father | *L.* | *pater:* father | paternal, paternity |
| **path** | feeling, disease | *L.* | *pathos:* suffering | sympathy, pathogenic |
| **patr** | father. *See* **pater** | | | patricide, patriotic |
| **pear** | show | *L.* | *parere:* show | appear, disappearance |
| **ped** | foot | *L.* | *pedalis:* foot | pedestrian, pedal |
| **ped** | child | *Gr.* | *paido:* child | pediatrician, pedology |
| **pel** | push | *L.* | *pellare:* to drive | expel, repel |
| **pen** | wrong | *L.* | *poena:* penalty | penalty, penalize |
| **pen** | sorry | *L.* | *paenitere:* repent | repent, penitent |
| **pend** | hang | *L.* | *pendere:* hang | pendant, dependent |
| **pent** | five | *Gr.* | *pente:* five | pentagon, pentad |
| **per-** | through | | | permit, perpetual |
| **peri-** | around | | | perimeter, periscope |
| **perso** | individual | *Gr.* | *persona:* mask | impersonal, personnel |
| **pet** | fight, struggle | *L.* | *petere:* strive | compete, petition |
| **pet** | go, toward | *L.* | *petere:* strive | repeat, perpetual |
| **petal** | move toward | *L.* | *petere:* seek | centripetal |
| **petro** | stone | *Gr.* | *petros:* stone | petroleum, petrology |
| **pharma** | drug | *Gr.* | *pharmakon:* drug | pharmacy, pharmaceutical |
| **phil** | love | *Gr.* | *philos:* loving | philosophy, philanthropy |
| **phobia** | fear | *Gr.* | *phobos:* fear | claustrophobia, acrophobia |
| **phon** | sound | *Gr.* | *phone:* sound | phonograph, phonetics |
| **photo** | light | *Gr.* | *phos-:* light | photograph, photogenic |
| **phys** | nature | *Gr.* | *phusikas:* nature | physical, physicist |
| **pire** | breathe. *See* **spir** | | | expire |
| **plac** | area, space | *L.* | *platus:* broad | replace, placement |
| **plain** | clear, level | *L.* | *planus:* clear | explain, plane |

| Word Element | Meaning | Etymology | Examples |
|---|---|---|---|
| plast | shape, mold | *Gr. plassein:* mold | plastic, plaster |
| plaud | noise | *L. plaudere:* clap | applaud, applause |
| plen, plete | full, fill | *L. plenus:* full | plenty, replete |
| plex, pli, plic | layer, involved | *L. plicare:* fold | complex, complicate |
| plod | noise. *See* **plaud** | | explode, implosion |
| plore | cry, disapprove | *L. plorare:* wail | deplore, implore |
| ploy | use, involve. *See* **plex** | | employ, deploy |
| plu | more than | *L. plus:* more | plural, plus |
| ply | fold, layer. *See* **plex** | | plywood, multiply |
| poin | point. *See* **punct** | | appoint, pointed |
| poli | smooth, polish | *L. polire:* polish | impolite, polished |
| polis | city, people | *Gr. polis:* city | political, metropolis |
| poly | many | *Gr. polus:* much | polyglot, polynomial |
| pon | set, place | *L. ponere:* place | postpone, opponent |
| pop | people | *L. populus:* people | popular, populace |
| por | hole | *Gr. poros:* passage | porous, pore |
| port | carry | *L. portare:* carry | portable, import |
| port | part | *L. portio:* part | portion, counterpart |
| pos | place, set. *See* **pon** | | impose, expose |
| poss | be able | *L. posse:* be able | possible, impossible |
| post- | after | | postpone, postgame |
| pot | power, force | *L. potens:* power | potent, potential |
| pound | place, set. *See* **pon** | | compound, expound |
| pow | power, force. *See* **pot** | | power, empowered |
| pre- | before | | predict, prepare |
| prec | value, worth | *L. pretium:* price | precious, depreciate |
| prehen | grasp, know | *L. prehendere:* seize | apprehend, comprehend |
| press | push, press | *L. pressare:* press | compress, pressure |
| pri, prim | first | *L. primus:* first | prime, primary |
| prin | first | *L. princeps:* first | principal, prince |
| pro- | before, forward | | progress, promote |
| prob | prove | *L. probare:* prove | probe, probation |
| propr | own, correct | *L. propire:* own | proper, property |
| proto- | first | | prototype, protoplasm |
| prov | test. *See* **prob** | | proved, improve |
| pseudo | false | *Gr. pseudes:* false | pseudonym |
| psych | mind | *Gr. psukhe:* soul | psychology, psychiatrist |
| pub | people | *L. publicus:* people | public, publicize |
| puls | push. *See* **pel** | | repulse, pulsate |

| Word Element | Meaning | Etymology | | Examples |
|---|---|---|---|---|
| **punct** | point, place | L. | *puncta:* pierced | puncture, punctual |
| **pur** | clean | L. | *purus:* clean | purify, impure |
| **pute** | think | L. | *putare:* think | compute, dispute |

# Q

| Word Element | Meaning | Etymology | | Examples |
|---|---|---|---|---|
| **quad** | four | L. | *quartus:* fourth | quadrangle, quadrant |
| **qual** | feature, property | L. | *qualitas:* kind | quality, disqualify |
| **quar** | four | L. | *quartus:* fourth | quarter, quartet |
| **quar** | ask, seek. *See* **qui** | | | quarrel |
| **que, qui** | look for, ask | L. | *quaerare:* seek | question, inquire |
| **quin** | five | L. | *quintus:* fifth | quintet, quintuplets |

# R

| Word Element | Meaning | Etymology | | Examples |
|---|---|---|---|---|
| **rab** | anger | L. | *rabere:* rave | rabid |
| **rad** | root, ray | L. | *radius:* ray | radiate |
| **rade** | rub, scratch | L. | *radere:* scrape | abrade, abrasion |
| **rag** | anger. *See* **rab** | | | raging, enrage |
| **rang** | order, line up | Fr. | *rengier:* line up | rank, arrange |
| **rase** | rub, scratch. *See* **rade** | | | erase, rash |
| **ratio** | reason, logic | L. | *ratio:* reason | rational, irrational |
| **rav** | anger. *See* **rab** | | | rave |
| **re-** | again, back | | | redo, regress |
| **real** | actual, true | L. | *realis:* in fact | reality, unrealistic |
| **rect** | straight, correct | L. | *rectus:* straight | correct, direct |
| **reg** | rule, control | L. | *regere:* direct | regulate, irregular |
| **religi** | belief, bond | L. | *religare:* tie back | religion, irreligious |
| **rend** | give | L. | *re + dare:* give back | surrender, rendition |
| **resid** | live | L. | *residere:* sit back | residence, nonresident |
| **retro-** | backward | | | retrofit, retrogress |
| **right** | correct | OE. | *riht:* right | righteous, rightful |
| **rob** | strong, support | L. | *robor:* strength | corroborate |
| **rod, ros** | destroy, break | L. | *rodere:* gnaw | corrosive, rodent |
| **roy** | rule. *See* **reg** | | | royal |
| **rupt** | break, burst | L. | *ruptus:* broken | erupt, disrupt |

| Word Element | Meaning | Etymology | Examples |
|---|---|---|---|
| **S** | | | |
| **sal** | salt | L. *salus:* salt | desalinate, salary |
| **sanct** | holy, sacred | L. *sanctus:* sacred | sanctuary, sanctify |
| **sapien** | wise, good sense | L. *sapere:* to be wise | sapient, *Homo sapiens* |
| **sat** | full, enough | L. *satis:* sufficient | satisfy, sated |
| **scend** | climb | L. *scandere:* climb | ascend, descent |
| **schol** | school | L. *schola:* school | scholar, scholarship |
| **sci** | knowledge | L. *scire:* know | science, conscious |
| **scope** | see | Gr. *skopien:* see | microscope, telescope |
| **scrib, scrip** | write | L. *scribere:* write | scribe, subscript |
| **se-** | away, apart, aside | | seclude, secede |
| **sec** | follow. *See* **sequ** | | consecutive |
| **sect, seg** | cut | L. *secare:* cut | section, intersect |
| **seismo** | shake | Gr. *seismos:* shake | seismograph |
| **sem** | seed | L. *semen:* seed | seminary, inseminate |
| **semble-** | same. *See* **simil** | | assemble, resemble |
| **semi-** | half | L. *semis:* half | semiannual, semiconductor |
| **sen** | old | L. *senex:* old | senile, senator |
| **sens, sent** | feel | L. *sentire:* feel | sensible, sentient |
| **sept** | rotten | Gr. *septos:* foul | antiseptic, septic |
| **sequ** | follow | L. *sequi:* follow | subsequent, sequel |
| **seri** | row, connect | L. *serere:* join | serial, series |
| **sert** | join | L. *serere:* join | desert, insert |
| **serve** | save | L. *servare:* keep | conserve, preserve |
| **serve** | aid, help | L. *servus:* slave | servant, servile |
| **sex** | six | L. *sex:* six | sextet, sextuplet |
| **-ship** | state of being | | hardship, friendship |
| **side** | to live in a place | L. *sidere:* sit | reside, preside |
| **sign** | mean | L. *signare:* sign | signify, signal |
| **simil-** | alike | L. *similis:* alike | similar, simulate |
| **simpl** | easy | L. *simplus:* simple | simplify, simplicity |
| **simul** | same. *See* **simil** | | simulate |
| **-sion** | state of being | | cohesion, adhesion |
| **sist** | remain, stand. *See* **stat** | | persist, insist |
| **soc** | people, group | L. *socius:* friends | social, society |
| **sol** | alone | L. *solus:* alone | solitude, solo |
| **somni** | sleep | L. *somnus:* sleep | somnambulant |
| **soni** | sound | L. *sonus:* sound | sonic, supersonic |

| Word Element | Meaning | Etymology | | Examples |
|---|---|---|---|---|
| **soph** | wise | *Gr.* | *sophos:* wise | philosophy, sophomore |
| **sorb** | suck, take in | *L.* | *sorbere:* suck | absorb, resorb |
| **soror** | sister | *L.* | *soror:* sister | sorority, sororicide |
| **spect** | watch, look at | *L.* | *spectare:* look at | spectator, spectacle |
| **speci** | type, kind | *L.* | *species:* type | specialize, specify |
| **sphere** | ball, globe | *L.* | *sphera:* globe | spheroid, hemisphere |
| **spir** | breathe | *L.* | *spirare:* breathe | inspire, spiritual |
| **spis** | look. *See* **spect** | | | despise |
| **spond** | answer, react | *L.* | *spondere:* promise | respond, despondent |
| **stab** | firm, standing | *L.* | *stabilis:* firm | stable, stabilize |
| **stal** | put, remain intact | *L.* | *stallum:* place | install, installation |
| **stat, stit** | remain, stand | *L.* | *stare:* stand | status, institute |
| **stim** | urge, arouse | *L.* | *stimulus:* goad | stimulate, stimulus |
| **strain, stren, stress, stric** | draw tight, bind | *L.* | *stringere:* tighten | strength, constrict |
| **stru, struct** | build | *L.* | *struere:* build | construct, destruction |
| **suad** | convince, urge | *L.* | *suadere:* urge | persuade, dissuade |
| **sub-** | under | | | subnormal, suppress |
| **sue** | follow. *See* **sequ** | | | pursue |
| **sup-** | under | | | suppress |
| **sui** | self | *L.* | *sui:* of one's self | suicide |
| **-sule** | little, small. *See* **cule** | | | capsule |
| **sum** | take | *L.* | *sumere:* take up | consume, resumption |
| **super-** | above | | | superior, superstructure |
| **sur-** | above, on top | | | surface, surmount |
| **sym, syn** | same, alike, together | | | sympathy, synonym |

# T

| Word Element | Meaning | Etymology | | Examples |
|---|---|---|---|---|
| **tach, tact** | touch | *L.* | *tactus:* touch | contact, tactile |
| **tail** | cut up | *Fr.* | *taillier:* cut up | retail, detail |
| **tain** | hold. *See* **ten** | | | contain, retainer |
| **tang** | touch | *L.* | *tangere:* touch | tangent, tangible |
| **tech** | skill, ability | *Gr.* | *tekne:* skill | technician, technical |
| **tele-** | far away | | | television, telephone |
| **temp** | time | *L.* | *tempus:* time | tempo, contemporary |

| Word Element | Meaning | Etymology | | Examples |
|---|---|---|---|---|
| **ten** | hold, keep | *L.* | *tenere:* hold | tenure, tenant |
| **tend, tens, tent** | stretch | *L.* | *tendere:* stretch | extend, tense, tent |
| **term** | limit, end | *L.* | *terminus:* boundary | terminal, terminate |
| **terr** | frighten, scare | *L.* | *terrere:* frighten | terrible, terrify |
| **terra** | earth, land | *L.* | *terra:* earth | terrain, mediterranean |
| **test** | fight, witness | *L.* | *testis:* witness | protest, contest |
| **theo** | god | *Gr.* | *theos:* god | theology, atheist |
| **theo** | knowledge | *Gr.* | *thea:* see | theory, theoretical |
| **therap** | help, aid | *Gr.* | *theraps:* helper | therapist, therapy |
| **thermo** | heat | *Gr.* | *thermos:* heat | thermal, thermojunction |
| **thes** | put together | *L.* | *tithenai:* put together | synthesis, antithesis |
| **-tion** | state of being | | | convention, toleration |
| **tol** | stand, bear | *L.* | *tolere:* bear | tolerate, intolerable |
| **tom** | cut | *Gr.* | *temnein:* cut | atom, epitome |
| **ton** | sound | *Gr.* | *tonos:* sound | monotone, toneless |
| **tors, tort** | twist, bend | *L.* | *torsus:* twisted | torsion, contort |
| **tox** | poison | *L.* | *toxicare:* poison | toxic, antitoxin |
| **tract** | pull | *L.* | *tractus:* pulled | contract, retract |
| **trans-** | across, from place to place, change | | | transfer, translate |
| **tri** | three | *L.* | *tres:* three | triangle, trinity |
| **trib** | give | *L.* | *tribuere:* give out | tribute, attribute |
| **troll** | roll, check | *L.* | *rotulus:* roll | controller |
| **troph** | develop, grow | *Gr.* | *trophe:* food | atrophy, hypertrophy |
| **trude, trus** | push, thrust | *L.* | *trudere:* thrust | intrude, extrusion |
| **-tude** | state of being | | | fortitude, rectitude |
| **turb** | confuse, mix up | *Gr.* | *turba:* confuse | perturb, disturb |
| **twi** | two. *See* **du** | | | twin, twilight |
| **typ** | form, style | *L.* | *typus:* form | atypical, typify |

# U

| Word Element | Meaning | Etymology | Examples |
|---|---|---|---|
| **under-** | down, lower | | underage, underfed |
| **uni** | one | *L. unus:* one | unite, unification |
| **-urb** | city | *L. urbanus:* city | suburban, urbane |
| **-ure** | state of being | | stature, fracture |
| **un-** | not | | uncertain, unreal |

| Word Element | Meaning | Etymology | Examples |
|---|---|---|---|
| **V** | | | |
| **vac** | empty, leave | *L. vacuus:* empty | vacate, vacuum |
| **vad** | fill, go | *L. vadere:* go | pervade, evade |
| **val** | worth, health | *L. valere:* be strong | devalue, valence |
| **van** | empty, leave | *L. vanus:* empty | vanish, vain |
| **vanq** | conquer, defeat. *See* **vinc** | | vanquish |
| **vant** | ahead, before | *L. avant:* in front of | advantage, *avant-garde* |
| **var** | change | *L. varius:* change | variety, variation |
| **vegi** | plant | *L. vegere:* enliven | vegetarian, vegetable |
| **ven** | come | *L. venire:* come | convene, prevent |
| **ventr** | stomach | *L. venter:* belly | ventriloquist |
| **ver** | true | *L. verus:* true | verify, verity |
| **verb** | word | *L. verbum:* word | verbal, adverb |
| **vere** | awe, respect | *L. verari:* wonder at | revere, irreverent |
| **vers, vert** | turn, change | *L. vertere:* to turn | reverse, divert |
| **via** | go, away | *L. via:* way | viaduct, previous |
| **vict** | conquer. *See* **vinc** | | victory, victorious |
| **vid** | see | *L. videre:* see | video, evident |
| **vig** | plant. *See* **vegi** | | vigor, invigorate |
| **vinc** | conquer, defeat | *L. vincere:* conquer | invincible, convince |
| **vir** | man | *L. vir:* man | virile, virility |
| **vis** | see. *See* **vid** | | vision, visible |
| **vit, viv** | life | *L. vita:* life | vital, revive |
| **voc** | call | *L. vocare:* call | vocal, revoke |
| **void** | empty. *See* **vac** | | void |
| **vok** | call. *See* **voc** | | invoke, revoke |
| **vole** | hope, wish | *L. volens:* wish | benevolent, malevolent |
| **volv** | roll, change | *L. volvere:* roll | revolve, evolve |
| **vor, vour** | eat | *L. vorare:* devour | voracious, herbivore |
| **voy** | see. *See* **vid** | | clairvoyant, voyeur |
| **Y** | | | |
| **-y** | full of, covered with | | rainy, icy |
| **Z** | | | |
| **zoo** | animal | *Gr. zoon:* animal | zoology, protozoa |